Original Visions

DENISE LARDNER CARMODY
JOHN TULLY CARMODY

UNIVERSITY OF TULSA

Original Visions

The Religions of Oral Peoples

MACMILLAN PUBLISHING COMPANY
NEW YORK

Maxwell Macmillan Canada
TORONTO

Maxwell Macmillan International
NEW YORK   OXFORD   SINGAPORE   SYDNEY

Editor: Maggie Barbieri
Production Supervisor: Jane O'Neill
Production Manager: Muriel Underwood

This book was set in New Baskerville and was printed and bound by Arcata
Graphics/Fairfield. The cover was printed by New England Book Components,
Inc.

Macmillan Publishing Company
866 Third Avenue, New York, New York 10022

Macmillan Publishing Company is part of the Maxwell Communication
Group of Companies.

Maxwell Macmillan Canada, Inc.
1200 Eglinton Avenue East
Suite 200
Don Mills, Ontario M3C 3N1

LIBRARY OF CONGRESS CATALOGING-IN-PUBLICATION DATA
Carmody, Denise Lardner, 1935–
    Original visions : the religions of oral peoples / Denise Lardner Carmody and
    John Tully Carmody.
        p.   cm.
    ISBN 0–02–319395–6 (pbk.)
    1. Religion, Primitive.   I. Carmody, John, 1939–.   II. Title.
    BL430.C38 1993
    291'.042—dc20   91–40740
                                                                         CIP

Printing: 1 2 3 4 5 6 7   Year: 3 4 5 6 7 8 9

For Jim Stewart

Preface

This book is an introductory text suitable for college courses on the religions of oral peoples—courses that a generation ago might have been entitled "Primitive Religions." We assume little background about world religions and take a humanistic approach, treating the native traditions of the Americas, Africa, and Australia as intriguing ways that fellow human beings have dealt with the great issues latent in their experience.

In general, our treatments stress the myths and rituals the peoples themselves have considered central to their way of life. We also provide a good deal of discussion on the nature of religious activity—the possible significance of what these peoples thought they were doing. As a baseline, and therefore as a way of suggesting comparisons across the vast range of data within the traditions that we treat, for each continental area we discuss native views of nature and society and of self and divinity. Orientational remarks occur in Chapter 1, and retrospective, summarizing remarks occur in our concluding chapter.

In addition to sources peculiar to each area of study, we have referred regularly to articles in *The Encyclopedia of Religion*, because this comprehensive overview is likely to be the best reference work available to college students.

Acknowledgments

It is a pleasant task to thank Helen McInnis of Macmillan Publishing Company for sponsoring this project, and also to thank the following readers whose comments helped us considerably: Norman Girardot, Lehigh University; Gary Knoppers, The Pennsylvania State University-Behrend; Alan M. Olson, Boston University, Daniel L. Pals, University of Miami; and Charles R. Strain, DePaul University.

Contents

CHAPTER 6

Conclusion   *99*

CHAPTER 1

Introduction

Original Visions

Consider the following account of a key experience in boyhood:

> Slowly I perceived that a voice was trying to tell me something. It was a bird cry, but I tell you, I began to understand some of it. That happens sometimes. I know a lady who had a butterfly sitting on her shoulder. That butterfly told her things. This made her become a great medicine woman.
>
> I heard a human voice too, strange and high-pitched, a voice which could not come from an ordinary, living being. All at once I was way up there with the birds. The hill with the vision pit was way above everything. I could look down even on the stars, and the moon was close to my left side. It seemed as though the earth and the stars were moving below me. A voice said, "You are sacrificing yourself here to be a medicine man. In time you will be one. You will teach other medicine men. We are the fowl people, the winged ones, the eagles and the owls. We are a nation and you shall be our brother. You will never kill or harm any one of us. You are going to understand us whenever you come to seek a vision here on this hill. You will learn about herbs and roots, and you will heal people. You will ask them for nothing in return. A man's life is short. Make yours a worthy one."[1]

The man reminiscing is Lame Deer, a Lakota (Sioux) medicine man. According to the tradition of his tribe, young men would go into the wilderness to a "vision pit" to seek a revelation that could direct their

---

[1] Joan Halifax, *Shamanic Voices* (New York: E. P. Dutton, 1979), 74–75.

lives. The message Lame Deer heard from the winged ones determined the course of his life. Although he had to work at many jobs—soldier, singer, radio clown, bootlegger—to survive, he defined himself as a medicine man. The core of his life was healing people—ministering to their sick bodies and spirits.

Consider another text, drawn from a scholarly work on Meso-american—traditional, pre-Christian Mexican—approaches to healing:

> The indigenous conception of illness made traditional medicine into an activity situated at the boundaries of religion, magic, and herbalism. The healer is, above all, a magician. Even while he is addressing the gods to ask for a cure, it is faith in his personal power that creates the belief that his prayer will be answered. When he uses hallucinogenic plants to go into a trance, he is straddling the boundary between magic and religion.
>
> Even though the Indians admit that a fault of the patient must have been at the origin of his illness, they believe no less that the onset of the pathological process is generally caused by the practice of malevolent magic. So the healer is engaged in a battle, and he will not triumph unless he is stronger than the one who casts the spells. He can then be content with curing the patient, but he may also be asked to send the malevolence back to its author, and there-by engage in an act of sorcery properly so-called. The power of the healer is thus ambivalent. It restores a person's balance, but may also destroy it. In the same way, despite his protestations, the heal-er is often taken for a sorcerer, which at times exposes him to reprisals.[2]

Here the focus is not on how healers obtain their vocations, but on how they function for their people. Both the healer and his or her peo-ple have to believe in personal power. Frequently, this power comes from "familiars"—animal spirits (like those who visited Lame Deer) that offer help. Healers may derive power from "magic," the effort to manipulate supernatural forces, to bend the gods or spirits to one's will. "Religion," by contrast, usually signifies bowing to the will of higher powers. Those who practice "herbalism," using plants to help in healing, know the local plant life and are experts in the healing properties of leaves, roots, and berries.

The healer can be involved in a battle. Many premodern peoples have thought of sickness as the work of an enemy. Those who hate the sick person have sent evil forces to attack. The healer therefore becomes a defender of the sick person, and, by extension, of the whole tribe, against

---

[2] Jacques Galinies *et al.*, "Cosmic Disorder, Illness, Death, and Magic in Mesoamerican Traditions," in *Mythologies*, comp. Yves Bonnefoy (Chicago: University of Chicago Press, 1991), 2: 1190.

such evil forces. Thus, the healer ought to be able to send evil against the enemies of the sick person, or the enemies of the entire tribe. One might call the effort to send evil power against enemies the work of a "sorcerer." We might also call such a person a bad medicine man, or a bad witch. We might even speak of "black magic," in contrast to the "white magic" of the good healer.

The terminology is less important than the overall picture of what many premodern peoples have thought sickness and healing involve. Their assumption has been that sickness is psychosomatic, that much more than physical affliction is involved. The spirit of the sick person is as important as his or her body, and the spirit of the healer has much to do with his or her ability to heal. The spirits of enemies might harm the sick person; nonhuman spirits, familiars of sorcerers, can be the agents of illness.

For the purposes of this book, "original visions" has two meanings. First, it suggests the kinds of experiences that healers such as Lame Deer typically received at the outset of their careers. The religious cultures of oral (nonliterate) peoples naturally involved more than healing, but the medicine-person (or shaman, to use an originally Central Asian term), who has often been the most important functionary in oral religions, was most prized for the ability to heal and so stand against evil. The visions that have empowered shamans, whether men or women, to serve their people comprise a complex worldview of dealing with spirits; this worldview is characteristic of a great deal of traditional, premodern religion.

Second, "original visions" also stands for the outlook that preceded modernity. Indeed, it calls to mind the first ways that human beings looked upon the world. In the next section we examine prehistoric religion, exploring what scholars think happened in the Stone Age, prior to "higher" civilizations. We call to mind the religions of all the peoples who lived without writing and the formalization of religious rituals to which writing contributed. These religions were original in the sense that they came first in humanity's evolution. They remain so in the sense that oral peoples, who are sometimes called "people of small-scale societies," have used them down to the present day to maintain a distinctive, fresh sense of the world.

When people live without written records, they tend to sense the world as coming to them fresh each day. Certainly, many oral peoples have prodigious memories and can organize their worlds exactly, in considerable detail, through complex mythologies or clusters of stories. Oral peoples thus have oral traditions, but they are not bound to texts. They do not have documents that remain unchanged from generation to generation. Their stories can be fixed, standardized, but not so firmly as stories committed to writing. To be sure, the interpretation of such documents tends to change, but literate people are held to something more objective than what oral people must honor. Notice, for example, the centrality of scriptural texts in literate religions: a scriptural text stands before the interpreter, an enormous voice commenting on the world.

So our venture into the religions of nonliterate peoples is likely to involve us in something more flexible than what we meet in literate cultures. In the shamans whom we study, the rituals and myths that we analyze, and even the gods that appear, we sense more "movement." If we allow ourselves to enjoy this movement, we can begin to appreciate the courage and humanity of our forebears. The people who dealt with sickness, death, beauty, injustice, and all the other great issues of human existence without scriptural records can remind us that, despite all our progress and literacy, we contemporary human beings still do not understand everything about creation. Things can still move for us, too, as our poets and mystics insist. When we recognize this fact, we come to understand that oral peoples have always been our sisters and brothers, much more like us than different.[3]

Prehistoric Peoples

The focus of this book is the oral peoples of historical, especially recent historical, times. Yet it is useful to consider oral peoples of prehistoric times, who are the ancestors of us all. The following description of Neanderthal skeletons gives us a sense of the lives of prehistoric peoples:

> Neanderthal skeletons often exhibit severe injuries, but for the most part we are not able to say with certainty whether they resulted from fights and battles. Some of the head injuries had healed; others were evidently fatal, and a hipbone of a man from a site on Mount Carmel [Israel] apparently has been pierced by some lancelike object. Not a few Neanderthals survived not only wounds but also numerous illnesses. This was apparent also from the skeleton of the original Neanderthal—the find that gave the Neanderthals their name—who despite numerous afflictions had reached the age of fifty or so, a very advanced age for his time. Evidence of illnesses is also observable in other finds, especially that of an elderly Neanderthal at Shanidar [Iraq] who was probably blind from childhood and whose right forearm had been amputated. He had survived a number of illnesses and injuries, something possible only if he enjoyed the protection and care of a community, although he was probably of little economic value to it. We have no way of knowing whether this man had other abilities and knowledge that might have made him a respected member of the group. In any case, this

---

[3] See Sam D. Gill, *Beyond the Primitive* (Englewood Cliffs, NJ: Prentice-Hall, 1982).

instance, as well as others, indicates that Neanderthals were by no means the crude savages that they are sometimes made out to be but lived in a kind of community in which not only the law of the jungle and economic utility carried weight."[4]

Neanderthals were an early line of Homo sapiens. They lived in the Paleolithic era, 35,000 to 85,000 years ago, long before the melting of the glaciers (perhaps 10,000 years ago). As the passage describes them, these people showed human traits. They may have made efforts at healing and judged the worth of individuals on other than utilitarian grounds. In other words, they probably showed respect for one another's spiritual qualities. People like the elderly Neanderthal of Shanidar who could be of little practical benefit to the tribe nevertheless received attention, perhaps at the sacrifice of time and resources.

Other evidence suggests that Neanderthals buried their dead carefully, in some cases with flowers. The significance to them of such burials is hard to say, but at the least they wanted the dead to lie with tokens of the beauty they had enjoyed during life. They may even have hoped that the dead would enter a new form of existence, where the beauty of flowers might resonate more than it had in the previous life with its many trials.

Though some scholars of prehistoric, Stone Age cultures think that religion has existed from the beginning of our species, others are dubious. The human species is defined by reflection. We are the only animals who can be both subject and object—can be aware of ourselves deliberately, in acts that objectify much of our sense of identity. One must therefore assume that the earliest human beings sensed that they existed in a world they did not control. With minds at least somewhat like our own, they could survey their habitats, even the heavens. They could wonder about birth and death, good fortune and bad. From Paleolithic cave paintings in Europe over 10,000 years old, we know that early human beings (whether Neanderthals or true members of our own line, Homo sapiens sapiens) were beguiled by the fertility of human beings and of animals and by the human need to hunt. Whether this wonder extended to the splendors and mysteries of creation we cannot say. But it is not impossible. Hunters and gatherers of recent times, the peoples whose way of life most approximates what we conjecture about prehistoric peoples of the Stone Age, show signs of possessing at least a vague sense of the sacred, the divine, an ultimate reality responsible for the way the world is constituted.

Marija Gimbutas, a leading paleontologist, has decoded various signs found in prehistoric remains in Central Europe that may be as much as 8,000 years old. She interprets them as indications of a widespread cult of a feminine deity:

---

[4] Karl J. Narr, "Paleolithic Religion," in *The Encyclopedia of Religion*, ed. Mircea Eliade (New York: Macmillan, 1987), 11: 151.

Chevrons, V's, zig-zags, M's, meanders, streams, nets, and tri-lines are frequent and repetitious Old European symbols. However, in all the literature on Neolithic and later ceramics they are considered to be just "geometric motifs"; the relation between design and symbol was not suspected. It took me years of detective work to discover how they were all related . . . [to] the symbols associated with the primary aspect of this Goddess, that of life-giving moisture of the Goddess's body—her breasts, eyes, mouth, and vulva. In these life-creating and protecting functions, her animal forms are ram, deer, bear, and snake. The latter also appears in an anthropomorphic shape and seems to be an alter ego of the Bird Goddess.[5]

Gimbutas's interpretation, which others have disputed or called highly speculative, links many decorations on such remains to a primordial female. She argues that early Europeans venerated the mysteries of life and death by associating them with women. The mystery of women bearing children never failed to fascinate them. Vegetation came forth from the earth somewhat as children came forth from their mother: where did *all* life come from? Perhaps the early Europeans envisioned a cosmic mother. Perhaps the earth symbolized a woman-like power from which all living things came forth and to which all returned at death. Burial, then, was like a return to the womb. All living things seemed to move back and forth, exiting from this womb and returning to it. The world might be a giant process of transmigration of the life-force.

The other aspects of female fertility—nursing, sexual excitement, menstruation—could be imagined as having cosmic dimensions. To stay on the good side of the life-giving force and to stay away from death, one might venerate cosmic femininity, the Great Goddess. Anything reminiscent of females—curves, cavities—could call the goddess to mind. Scholars have found numerous figurines depicting pregnant women, usually without faces, as though to suggest a universal, impersonal force. For prehistoric peoples, survival was the paramount need, so everything bearing on survival—fertility, birth, food, healing—drew their passionate, and one could say religious, interest.

Recent Oral Peoples

Throughout the millennia that separate peoples of the twentieth century from prehistoric people of the Neolithic era, human beings continued to be preoccupied with survival. If a few civilizations flourished, making life relatively secure for the majority of their people, many peoples remained on the edge of survival, struggling generation after generation. The cul-

---

[5] Marija Gimbutas, *The Language of the Goddess* (San Francisco: Harper & Row, 1989), 3.

tures that lie between us and the Neolithic era exhibit a wide variety of divine beings, no doubt because many different forces seemed involved in survival. People prayed to gods and goddesses, followed the sun and the moon, venerated "masters of the animals" (deities thought responsible for wild game), and relied on key forces like the wind and the rain. Sometimes tribes generalized their sense of the powers that held their fate, speaking of "earth" or "heaven" or even a holy power such as "the Great Spirit." Often they sent their petitions and thanksgivings in various directions; as venerators of many different gods, they were "polytheistic."

For many recent peoples a sacred femininity continued to be important. As one of the Kagaba of what is now Colombia put it:

> The mother of our songs, the mother of all our seed, bore us in the beginning of things and so she is the mother of all types of men, the mother of all nations. She is the mother of the thunder, the mother of the streams, the mother of trees and of all things. She is the mother of the world and of the older brothers, the stone-people. She is the mother of the fruits of the earth and of all things. She is the mother of our youngest brothers, the French and the strangers. She is the mother of our dance paraphernalia, of all our temples, and she is the only mother we possess. She alone is the mother of the fire and the Sun and the Milky Way. . . . She is the mother of the rain and the only mother we possess. And she has left us a token in all the temples . . . a token in the form of songs and dances.[6]

The Mother is generalized; everything comes from her. The avowal that she is "the only mother we possess" sounds like a profession of faith: To her, our best god and ultimate source of help, do we commit ourselves.

The Kagaba, like many other Native Americans, think of the nonhuman orders of existence as people. Just as Lame Deer spoke of the winged people, the speaker here refers to "the stone people"—the rocks, boulders, mountain crags. As everything comes from a single source, and everything has being, all is kin to human beings.

The notion that everything comes from a single source and possesses the same essential being allows many oral peoples to feel at home in the world. Even frightening beings have a valid status. The Mother or the gods made them, too, so they are not completely foreign, not independent agents. Inasmuch as oral peoples have tended to personify these forces, their world has been full of "people." However differently a stone might think and will, the typical tribe of an oral, small-scale culture considered it worthy of respect. It might not have the spontaneity of living things, but it did not die. Indeed, when they speculated about immortality, many oral peoples used images involving stone: Graves might be cut into stone. Stones could be considered the bones of Mother Earth. One

---

[6] Mircea Eliade, *From Primitives to Zen* (New York: Harper & Row, 1967), 16.

could memorialize a great chief by building a stone pillar. If one wanted to placate the spirits of a place, one could add a stone to the cairn created by other passersby. Because stones had a powerful kind of fertility, one that lasted for eons, women wanting to conceive might press against them. A stone hammer was a preferred way of dispatching the dying to the next life.[7]

Oral peoples of recent times have continued to hand down intuitions about the natural world that shaped the lives of prehistoric peoples. Although fewer and fewer peoples could avoid the influence of literate cultures, in remote regions—and even among European peasants—many centuries-old beliefs persisted into the early twentieth century. The less literate people were, and the more directly dependent on nature, the more they resembled Neolithic, even Paleolithic, peoples. Their sense of the world came to them through oral traditions. Relatively little technology, in our modern sense of the term, stood between them and nature.

In one interpretation of the ancient oral mentality, what we now call "critical reason" had not precipitated out from a generalized intelligence, so there was no science—no fully disciplined, rationalized experimentation or control of experience. Thus, dreams could be as significant as waking impressions—perhaps more, because more extraordinary. The criterion of reality tended to be vivid experience. If a vision or dream made a person's hair stand on end, or lent an aura of serenity, or presented an unearthly beauty, it counted as extremely important. The gods could speak through many different means. Birds could carry messages, the wind moving through the corn could be spirits singing.

When they first encountered this ancient oral mentality, modern Western observers characterized it as "primitive" compared to our own "sophistication." We have books, science, high technology. The natives of small, nonliterate tribes had only lovely stories and some quaint and not so quaint customs. The one expression of humanity is fully adult, the other represented the childhood, or at best the adolescence, of human potential.

However, as investigators learned more about oral cultures, such first impressions were revised. Many peoples can be considered undeveloped in terms of science, technology, medicine, economics; but most are highly developed in terms of art, mythology, dance, and wisdom about the human condition. Meditations on death, its origin and significance, abound in oral cultures. Again and again, oral peoples wrestle with the painful mystery that human beings must suffer and die. Similarly, they wrestle with evil, with what should not be, including all the wrongs human beings inflict on one another. Yet balancing this fascination with death and evil is a great affirmation of life. Lack of writing has not meant lack of wisdom, or beauty, or holiness, or love. In fact, lack of writing

---

[7] See Mircea Eliade, *A History of Religious Ideas* (Chicago: University of Chicago Press, 1978), 1: 114–120.

could mean being free to let natural beauty, or inner silence, or human speech reach one's spirit directly. Song and dance, art and music tend to flourish in oral cultures, sometimes along with a leisure that people of contemporary, technological societies might envy. Poor material conditions do not preclude profound prayer, or meaningful interaction. Much of the value that one places on a culture depends on the criteria that one imposes. If one values spiritual satisfactions—celebrating life, appreciating beauty, sharing honesty and love—oral peoples can indeed seem highly developed.

If nothing else, the ecological crisis that modern technology has created suggests that oral peoples have much to teach us. They have lived in relative harmony with nature for tens of thousands of years. They have not needed vast hordes of material possessions. Certainly, if offered modern conveniences, many of them rush forward to take them. Yet even as oral peoples have conceded that accommodation to modern, Western technology is inevitable, traditional Africans and Americans, Asians and Australians have worried about what they fear they are sure to lose. Their myths and rituals are precious, as are their family ties. Their ability to interact with nature spontaneously, finding it full of wonders, seems a large price to pay for "progress."

There have been countless debates about colonialism, the preservation of native cultures, and traditional patterns of religious and sexual mores. Part of the value of studying oral peoples is to force ourselves to listen to their ideas about human existence, to acknowledge that there are many different ways of defining "prosperity," "achievement," and "development."

This Book

The scope of this book is the four major groups of recent oral peoples: Native North Americans, Native Latin Americans, Native Africans, and Native Australians and South Sea Islanders. In each area hundreds of different tribes have evolved. Obviously, we cannot consider them all, but we can point to thematic connections, which tend to be immersed in traditional mythologies. We deal then, with many colorful stories, and each story implies an original vision. Though some stories developed from the storyteller's delight in making events unfold, we must accept the fact that traditional peoples regarded established, consecrated stories as true reports.

Such truth was not always the literal truth as established by modern science, nor did it mirror the modern historian's effort to reproduce or picture the past exactly as it occurred. Rather, the truth of the stories of traditional oral peoples was the insight such stories afforded. The stories helped people sense how the world was constructed. They offered hints about how to proceed in the world, how to act prudently and wisely. And they often bestowed the comfort of having been used and revered by pre-

vious generations. Traditional myths may evolve generation by generation, but usually the central myths of a people have been handed down
through time out of mind. Knowing that many ancestors had profited
from them, oral peoples could be confident that taking them to heart
would bring great benefit.

The traditional oral peoples of North, Central, and South America all
seem to have come from East Asia. The basic parent stock is what ethnologists call Mongoloid. Whether all natives of the Americas descend from
immigrants who tens of thousands of years ago crossed a land bridge
connecting the shores now divided by the Bering Strait is not certain.
People may have arrived by boat from Asia, landing at various points
along the West Coast of the Americas. Still, the relative sameness of ethnological characteristics of Native Americans suggests that they share
both genetic endowment and an original cultural endowment.

However differently particular tribes have developed, because of vary-
ing patterns of evolution, migration, and adaptation to different habitats,
certain inclinations reappear regularly. For example, most of the tribes
have sponsored some form of ecstatic activity—shamanism, or moving
from ordinary consciousness to states of trance or special perception. All
tribes have told myths and enacted rituals—dances, ceremonies, physical
expressions of the myths. Nature has been the great wonder of all tribes.
The distinctions that we Westerners now make among physical nature,
the human self, the human social group, and divinity have been less clear
to traditional Native Americans. The world has been a living unity, with
divisions among different creatures only partial and provisional. Basic
economies were built on hunting and gathering, though in many places
farming developed. Only in the empires of Central America and the
Andes of South America were large numbers of people organized. And
only in those empires was there an elaborate division of labor—a sophisticated priesthood, a military, and so on—and such features as a system
of trade, a calendar, astrology, and architecture.

Traditional Africans and Australians also vary considerably among
themselves. Africa seems to have been the home of the human species,
which arose millions of years ago. Estimates of the age of the human
presence in Australia vary, with 25,000 years a conservative judgment.
Natives of both continents have been shamanistic; Native Australians
refer to trances as the "dream time." Although of different racial stock
from that of natives of the Americas, these other traditionally oral peoples have also told stories, elaborated rituals, and considered ceremonies
to be as significant as physical means of survival—hunting, gathering,
farming. Their worldviews have also been characterized by a holistic
approach to nature, the self, the human social group, and divinity. With
fewer significant exceptions than in the Americas, we cannot speak of
empires or extended civilizations.

Though our focus is on relatively recent oral peoples, we cannot avoid questions of history or longstanding practice. By surveying representative tribes, myths, and rituals, we indicate how the people of a given area probably thought about the physical world, the individual self, the social group, and ultimate reality—the gods or spirits held responsible for the rise and structuring of the world. Beneath the great diversity of stories and symbols, a few central, recurrent themes suggest the parameters of the native worldview: questions of life and death, the origin of key cultural features, the patterns of time (origins and endings), sexuality, and relations with plants and animals. By exploring these themes, Native Americans, Africans, and Australians can become less exotic than they may first seem.

Human beings everywhere have been involved in the same basic tasks: warding off death and disease, searching for meaning, celebrating the goodness of human existence, and defending one another against its ills. All human beings die. All suffer. None know with empirical certainty how the world arose, where human beings go at death, why there is suffering, injustice, evil, beauty, truth, love. Therefore, all tribes, larger groups, and even empires have been engaged in a twofold project: physical survival and spiritual satisfaction—bread and roses. This project remains with us today. What can we learn from oral peoples? What bearing does *their* learning have on what we now do? Such questions make religious studies deeply humanistic.

Study Questions

1. How did Lame Deer's vision affect his life?
2. How have traditional oral peoples tended to think about sickness and healing?
3. What is the significance of prehistoric peoples' having sometimes buried their dead with flowers?
4. Of what interest to prehistoric peoples was female fertility?
5. What lies behind oral peoples' veneration of stone?
6. What is the significance of vivid experience in the lives of oral peoples?
7. Speculate on the significance of possessing a similar genetic endowment with that of living in a different habitat.
8. What is meant by "ecstatic experiences"?

CHAPTER 2

Native North Americans

Overview

In this chapter we consider Native North Americans from all the major geographical areas: the Far North, the Eastern Woodlands, the Central Plains, the Northwest coast, California, the region between the Rockies and the Sierra and Cascade ranges, and the Southwest. Virtually everywhere, tribes were small. A large settlement, such as those that sometimes developed in the southeast woodlands, numbered 1,000 people. What we know about Native Americans since "historical" times, or since contact with whites began in the sixteenth century, suggests that hunting and gathering was more typical than farming. Still, in the southeast and the southwest farming prevailed. Methods of survival depended on both the local habitat and the traditions with which tribes of a given area were in contact; for example, Central American traditions apparently had considerable influence on southeast and southwest tribes.

Though the earliest settlers to this continent may have arrived tens of thousands of years ago, giving ample time for different traditions to develop, two characteristics of North American religious traditions remain constant: (1) an interest in visions and (2) an elaborate ceremonial life.[1]

Lame Deer's account of the vision that determined he would be a medicine man is typical of what many tribes sought. More young men than women pursued visions at puberty because the power that women needed to be mothers came naturally. But in some tribes women could also pursue visions. Even after a successful vision-quest at the gateway to

---

[1] See Ake Hultkrantz, "North American Religions: An Overview," in *The Encyclopedia of Religion*, ed. Mircea Eliade (New York: Macmillan, 1987), 10: 526.

adulthood, however, Native North Americans could continue to seek illumination.

For example, shamans needed visions to work successfully as healers, as did people charged with determining where the game had wandered, psychopomps (people empowered to lead the dead to their place of rest), and diviners (people who could predict the future). To free their spirits they learned techniques such as dancing, singing, beating drums, ingesting tobacco or hallucinogens such as peyote, fasting, immersing themselves in frigid water, abstaining from sexual relations, and staring at skeletons. Once free, their spirits could travel in search of game, or to find the keeper of the animals and bargain with him or her to release the game, or to find the evil spirit that had caused an illness, or to follow the spirit of a dead person to the land of rest.

Other members of the tribe might also seek visions. Sometimes the reason was practical: the vision could answer a problem such as to whom to marry a daughter, or whether to vote for war. Other times the reason was aesthetic and religious: the seeker wanted to see beauty, find meaning, contact the sacred. People who live in cultures that prize visions tend to report that, over time, moving outside of ordinary awareness—refreshing one's sense of the wonders of the cosmos, or the holiness of the deities, or the power of the spirits guiding tribal life—becomes an habitual need. Such people develop a positive addiction for contact with a world, a reality, that seems more significant than that revealed in ordinary, frequently dull, daily affairs.

Pueblo Indians of the American Southwest have sometimes meditated daily, focusing on the rising and setting of the sun. To greet the sun at dawn could be understood as a contribution to keeping the world going. Without human attention to sunrise, praise of the sun's great beauty, the miracle might cease to occur. In addition to the aesthetic dimension of witnessing sunrise and sunset, such Indians have found in it a religious focus: The sun stands for light and warmth, for divine providence, for care, guidance, and nurture.

The Native American devotion to the sun did not preclude devotion to the earth as well. Both served the needs of the tribe and therefore both deserved thanksgiving. Mother Earth was the source of crops, such as maize and beans, on which the tribe depended. And certainly, one also had to pray for rain. But admiring the sun each day, meditating on its beauty and power, could focus a person's spirit and usher in a profound peace. It could become a habitual source of satisfaction, especially when it grew to be less a matter of words or ideas than a matter of love, communion, and contemplation.

The second characteristic of Native American religious life is the use of ceremony for significant occasions. We see this, for example, in the Lakota use of the sweatlodge and the sacred pipe. On any significant occasion both men and women might use the sweatlodge to purify themselves. The lodge was a hut built to enclose a pile of stones that were heated, then doused with water to produce steam. Sitting naked in the hut, one sweated out bodily impurities, thereby helping one's spirit cleanse itself.

Because Native American thought is holistic, affirming the close relationship between body and spirit, the experience of bodily cleansing served as a metaphor for spiritual purification. Emerging from the sweatlodge, the person felt renewed; the challenge was to retain the sense of purity the sweatlodge had produced. Several important Lakota myths teach the danger of not approaching holy things in the right spirit. For example, when one of a pair of young men, seeing the Buffalo Lady, source of the key cultural gifts of the Lakota, desires her carnally, he is wrapped in a cloud; when the cloud lifts the other man sees only his friend's bones.

The ceremonial for the sweatlodge usually invited all of nature to partake in the process of purification and prayer that the users carried out. People would throw a bit of grass on the stones or into the air to let the land participate. In both the sweatlodge and other rituals, the sacred pipe, filled with tobacco, was more than an instrument for social bonding. The yield of the land that filled the pipe, giving it its sweet smoke and satisfying effect on the body, reminded the smokers that Mother Earth was their constant benefactor. The rising of the smoke toward the heavens symbolized the rising of spirit desired by devout natives.

The goal of Native American ceremonies was to send oneself to "the Great Spirit" watching over things from the sky. This Spirit, usually pictured as a cosmic Father, was the source of the rains that fertilized Mother Earth, the winds that either cooled or froze things, the sun that either warmed or seared them. And the materials used to make the pipe—animal bones and rocks—represented the other ranks of creation. Native Americans felt themselves to be a part of a "democratic" cosmos. As many fellow beings shared the earth with them, it was only right to include these beings in sacred ceremonies. If ceremonial prayers became a great chorus of praise for the Great Spirit rising from all his creatures, they could only be more effective.[2]

As we study the myths and rituals of natives of various parts of North America, we see that at the heart of a given culture was the sense of sacredness, of profound meaning. To be sure, Native Americans, like all human beings, have had to secure food and shelter, to care for children, to engage in practical tasks. But they prized spiritual significance over material bounty. Again and again, we see them setting aside parts of the year to rehearse their myths and celebrate their festivals. The measure of a person was based on wisdom and courage, a power stemming from intercourse with the holy spirits at work invisibly in the cosmos.

---

[2] See Joseph Epes Brown, *The Sacred Pipe* (Baltimore: Penguin, 1971).

Natives of the Far North

The peoples of the Far North show the greatest similarity to the Asian peoples, whom ethnologists hypothesize are the historical parents of Native Americans. Indeed, it is difficult to distinguish the Inuit (Eskimos) of the polar regions into Asian and North American peoples. For both, adapting to harsh physical conditions has been the key to survival. It has also been the key to religious culture.

The economy of the far northern tribes has always been one of hunting and fishing. In summer the people might gather berries or roots in addition to collecting fish eggs and nestlings, but for the rest of the year animals and fish were the key sources of food. Thus, tribes tended to follow the caribou, or the reindeer, or the seals. Because of the nomadic life that this entailed, Inuit became experts at erecting quick housing and developing a portable economy. Many observers have marveled at their technology, which, though in some ways very simple, was ingeniously adapted to local conditions. Traditional clothing, for example, continues to outperform most alternatives manufactured by whites. The use of dogs (perhaps originally tamed wolves) is another remarkable achievement. Seals and walruses have served some tribes as comprehensively as buffalo served tribes of the central plains. Women would spend weeks chewing the skins of seals to soften them so they could be worked into garments. Furs had to be fitted with great skill. This practical, economic activity flowed from a view of the world now on the verge of oblivion—that of the hunter, bred over generations for extreme sensitivity to any shift in the environment.

Barry Lopez, a writer about nature who spent time in the early 1980s with Arctic peoples struggling against many threats to their native way of life, identifies at the center of their culture a sense of the land, the environment, that a white observer can barely imagine:

> Land-use-and-occupancy projects have been conducted by and with native peoples throughout the Arctic, in furtherance of their land claims and to protect their hunting rights. These studies have revealed a long and remarkably unbroken connection between various groups of indigenous people and the particular regions of the Arctic they inhabit. It is impossible to separate their culture from these landscapes. The land is like a kind of knowledge traveling in time through them. Land does for them what architecture sometimes does for us. It provides a sense of place, of scale, of history; and a conviction that what they most dread—annihilation, eclipse—will not occur. "We are here because our ancestors are real," a man once told an interviewer. The ancestors are real by virtue of their knowledge and use of the land, their affection for it. A native woman, alone and melancholy in a hospital room, told another

interviewer she would sometimes raise her hands before her eyes to stare at them. "Right in my hand, I could see the shorelines, beaches, lakes, mountains, and hills I had been to. I could see the seals, birds, and game."[3]

Lopez suggests that Arctic peoples have connatural knowledge of the land—a knowledge not born of facts or concepts but of inborn, intuited connections. Mother and child have a connatural knowledge of one another, as do lovers. Mystics have a connatural knowledge of God; the expression of what they "know" might seem nothing but babble, yet they are no less certain of its truth. Native peoples have lived with the land so intimately, so totally, for so many generations that it forms them. Their selves are so profoundly tied up with the land they have walked, the land in which they have struggled, that they cannot identify themselves apart from it. If forcibly removed, as were many Native Americans of more southerly regions by whites in the nineteenth century, they were likely to languish. Nothing physical was lacking—not food or shelter or medicine—only their spiritual home, but that lack was powerful enough to squelch their will to live.

Many other aspects of traditional life in the Far North come alive when we place them in the context of fierce attachment to the land. Eskimos have been some of the most dramatic spiritual travelers and ascetics; their stark forms of shamanism mirror the starkness of the land. The relative poverty of their myths mirrors the bareness, the all-whiteness, of the land much of the year. A great wariness runs through Inuit culture, leading to many taboos. The fear of blood; the stricture to placate the spirits of slain animals; and a worry as to the unappeased spirits of departed ancestors all reflect an environment in which death can come at any moment. Let the ice break, the blizzard blow in, the child be exposed to the elements for five minutes, and all can be lost. Let people talk too much, not pay attention, and precious game can escape, starvation threaten.

A leading Inuit myth is that of the origin of the sea animals from the fingers of the goddess Sedna. Sedna was a proud girl who married a sea-bird. The marriage went badly, so she wanted to end it. Her father helped her, but as they were escaping, a flock of sea-birds threatened them. As a storm blew up, Sedna was tossed from the boat. She clung to the side but her father, in his panic to escape, chopped off her fingers. From them came the seals and other animals of the sea. Enraged, Sedna eventually sent her great dog to gnaw off her father's feet. She got her revenge, but also a further punishment. For the impiety of attacking her parent, she was banished to the ocean floor. There she rules with her dreadful dog, controlling the sea animals. Often she becomes ill-tem-

---

[3] Barry Lopez, *Arctic Dreams* (New York: Scribner's, 1986), 164–165.

pered because her long hair snarls, and she shuts up the sea animals, giving the Inuit no game. The shaman has to go into a trance, travel to the bottom of the sea, skirt her dog, and persuade her to let him comb out her hair. Then she may relent and release the game.[4]

We can never know whether the average person took a myth such as this to be literal. Perhaps the symbolism was more important than the details. Though the details could remain etched in the exact memory for stories that oral peoples often exhibit, the details tended to be less important than the overall message. The message of this myth clearly entailed such staples of Inuit culture as the intimacy between human beings and animals (symbolized by the derivation of the sea animals from the body of the human female Sedna), the caprice of the forces running the world (the ill temper that could come over Sedna), the dark streak in parent-child relations (the tension between Sedna and her father), and the precarious bond between human beings and both the animal world and the familiars who came in visions and were supposed to provide guidance (perhaps symbolized by the marriage between Sedna and the sea-bird).

The usual explanation of Sedna's ill temper was that the tribe had broken taboos. These might be rules for how to treat game, or social rules such as prohibitions on incest or abortion. Keeping harmony with nature, with the forces running the physical world, was the key to survival and prosperity. When things went badly, it was assumed that disharmonies had arisen. Human beings had a great responsibility to attune themselves to the spirits running the physical world. Nothing positive could happen—no successful hunt, no healthy birth, no good feelings between men and women—without their approval. Practical human efforts were certainly important—skill was required of those who hunted, those who sewed, and so on. But observing taboos and supporting the shaman in his struggles to help the tribe were equally important, because they were all that human beings could do to enlist the most crucial help—that of the spirits. The most skillful hunter could fail because sometimes no game appeared. The most careful kayaker could fail because the ice could close around what had been open water, trapping him fatally. Exposed to the elements, naked before the onslaught of storms, natives of the Far North needed spiritual power—the sense that they could wrestle with the ultimate forces and wring from them wisdom sufficient to ensure another generation.

Natives of the Eastern Woodlands

The Eastern Woodlands encompasses a vast geographical area. From eastern Canada in the north to Florida in the south, woodlands were the

---

[4] See Franz Boas, *The Central Eskimo* (Lincoln: University of Nebraska Press, 1964), 175.

habitat for thousands of Native North Americans with a great variety of tribes and languages. Peoples of this area lived by hunting and gathering, though in the centuries prior to contact with whites some groups in the southeast cleared land and farmed.

The Winnebago lived south of the Great Lakes, and so close to some Plains tribes. Their belief in reincarnation may have been a Plains influence. Wars between tribes tended to follow language groups: Even though tribes were small, when they spoke kindred tongues and could understand one another they composed a sort of nation. Tribes were most likely to battle other tribes they could not understand, and in some wars tribes would band together with linguistic cousins. For the Winnebago elder who here addresses his son, warfare is a noble business:

> It is good to die on the warpath. If you die in war, your soul will not become unconscious. You will then be able to do what you please with your soul. Your soul will always remain in a happy condition. If you choose to go back to earth as a human being and live again you can do so. You can live a second life on earth or live in the form of those who walk on the light [the birds], or in the form of an animal, if you choose. All of these benefits will you obtain if you die in battle.
>
> If you have not obtained war blessings, fast for your position in life. If you fast in this way, after you get married you will get along well. You will then not have to worry about having children nor about your happiness. If you dream of your home, throughout life you shall be in want of nothing. Fast for food you are to receive. If you fast often enough for these things, then some day when your children ask for food, they will be able to obtain without difficulty a piece of deer meat, or perhaps even a piece of moose meat. You have it within you to see to it that your children shall never be hungry.[5]

War is one of the main things that men do, along with hunting. Whereas men are in the business of killing, women are in the business of nourishing life. Thus it can be important to separate men and women, lest their businesses—the powers that nature has given them—collide. To die in warfare in behalf of the tribe is a blessed death. Virtually all martial peoples have preached a doctrine like this to justify their battles and losses. For the Winnebago, the dignity of death in battle derives from the control of the soul, the animating spirit, that the fallen warrior gains. The Winnebago believed that transmigration was not inevitable. Only people with enough power could control their return to earth in new forms. Because the warrior had confronted death bravely he had wrested power from it.

Descriptions of Native American "theology," as we might call native ideas about the ultimate powers running the world, range from an

---

[5] Elisabeth Tooker, ed., *Native North American Spirituality of the Eastern Woodlands* (New York: Paulist Press, 1979), 73–74.

impersonal ultimate being like Time, to the Great Spirit, sometimes pictured as a kindly yet powerful grandfather or grandmother.

In the words of one scholar,

> Religion among the Indian tribes of the eastern woodlands is
> reported to include the concept of an All-Father of the type of [the
> Norse god] Odin or [the Greek god] Zeus . . . The Indians of the
> great forests . . . postulated a supreme being, all-embracing, but
> without form and having little contact with men. The concept was
> more like an abstract notion such as Time, thought of as the bearer
> of fore-ordained events. For most people this Great Manitou, or
> Spirit, was an ever present emotive force that took second place to
> the world of nature spirits who were concerned with daily affairs."[6]

Probably the ultimate reality for natives of the woodlands comprised
both impersonal and personal aspects—from time, space, the weather,
the animals, to shamans and warriors, mothers and children. The concept of power can include the ability to charm, lure, strengthen, support,
astonish, fill with joy. Tribes of the Eastern Woodlands respected this
power and sought it. When they thought about the creator of the world,
he/she/it was full of a many-sided power.

Natives of the Plains

The Plains Indians have been the object of much study. Indeed, probably
the most famous are the Lakota (Sioux), known for their sun dance, and
for the description of their traditional beliefs and rites offered by their
seer Black Elk.[7] The words of an old Omaha offer an excellent illustra-
tion of the kinship with other creatures that figures prominently in
Native American religion:

> When I was a youth, the country was very beautiful. Along the rivers
> were belts of timberland, where grew cottonwood, maple, elm, ash,
> hickory and walnut trees, and many other shrubs. And under these
> grew many good herbs and beautiful flowering plants. In both the
> woodland and the prairies I could see the trails of many kinds of
> birds. When I walked abroad I could see many forms of life, beauti-
> ful living creatures which *Wakananda* [the Great Spirit] had placed
> here; and these were, after their manner, walking, flying, leaping,
> running, playing all about. But now the face of all the land is

---

[6] Cottie Burland, *North American Indian Mythology* (London: Paul Hamlyn, 1975),
55.

[7] See Brown, *The Sacred Pipe*; also John Neihardt, *Black Elk Speaks* (Lincoln:
University of Nebraska Press, 1961).

changed and sad. The living creatures are gone. I see the land desolate and I suffer an unspeakable sadness. Sometimes I wake in the night and I feel as though I should suffocate from the pressure of this awful feeling of loneliness.[8]

Can a modern Western person appreciate this man's loss? If one has never considered nonhuman creatures brothers and sisters, is it possible to feel such loneliness? The Omaha speaks from a preindustrial, predevelopmental mentality. He has not been trained to think that God stands apart from the world, or that nature ought to be feared. But an overconcentration on the human side of creation, a twisting of nature to serve human needs, has eliminated the most precious things in his world.

Traditional Plains tribes celebrated the natural elements in such rituals as the sweatlodge. The six directions (above and below, in addition to north, south, east, and west), with their winds and vistas, along with the different orders of beings (birds, rocks, large animals, small animals, fish, grasses, trees), entered into their prayers. The more attuned they were to their surroundings, the more constantly they conversed with these fellow creatures. Certainly, they were not ecological saints. On occasion they abused fellow creatures by overhunting, overfishing, damaging land and moving on. They also slaughtered members of other tribes. But that was the exception, not the rule. The rule was that the land, and its cornucopia of creatures, had a value in its own right, apart from its utility for human beings. The rule was that one respected the souls of the animals one hunted (on the Plains, particularly buffalo), revered the earth on which one trod. Thus the whites' subjugation of the land seemed a profanation. The damage inflicted on the ecosphere caused visceral pain. Native Americans did not think of financial losses because they did not think of the land as personal property. They grieved over the devastation of holy beings, sacred sites, presences of the Great Spirit. And they found that their losses were incalculable. An entire way of life was wiped out.

Two rituals important on the Plains were the Hako and the sun dance. The Hako was a ceremony to promote health and prosperity. From it tribes hoped to gain numerous children, protection against sickness, long life, happiness, peace, vigor, and other victories over illness and infertility. The songs and dances associated with the Hako lay in the keeping of the tribal elders. Each gesture and prayer had a venerable history, was sacred and had to be enacted carefully, reverently. The more exactly the people performed the Hako, the better the chance that it would bring its intended effects. The usual time for the Hako was spring, when life was stirring, but it could also be celebrated in fall, when the birds were heading south.

---

[8] Reported in Melvin R. Gilmore, *Prairie Smoke* (New York: Columbia University Press, 1929), 36; quoted in Joseph Epes Brown, *The Spiritual Legacy of the American Indian* (New York: Crossroad, 1982), 40.

A special tie to the birds suggests the spiritual dimensions of this ceremony. The flight of birds regularly connotes the movement of the human spirit toward the holy powers. At the close of the Hako, the elders would bless the younger members of the tribe with feathered wands. These instruments were the emblems of the Hako, and so of good health. Thus, to give a feathered wand to an enemy was a way of making peace. Relations among friends that had sickened could be restored to health. The feathered wand also became a symbol of good relations between the generations.

The more famous sun dance usually occurred in early summer in conjunction with the buffalo hunt. The tribe would construct a circle of trees to represent the fullness of the people and the bounty of nature. The essence of the ceremony was for men to dance for several days gazing at the sun. They were offering themselves, their energy and pain, for the welfare of the people. To increase their pain, and so the merit of their offering, they would tie leather thongs to the trees and then fix them to their own breasts. As they danced the thongs would pull through their flesh and tear it. Because everything else in the world already belonged to the Great Spirit, the offering of human flesh was especially significant. Human beings had dominion over their own bodies; to offer themselves was the best of gifts.

Native American culture, like traditional cultures the world over, placed more stress on the group than on the individual. The individual existed to serve the group and insure its survival. The sacrifices made by warriors, hunters, and women in childbirth all aimed at the welfare of the group. That is not to say that Native Americans allowed no personal satisfactions, or that they did not value different interests and talents. But nothing was more important than benefiting the tribe. Everything was geared to promoting the survival and future of one's people.

Natives of the Northwest

In this section we consider tribes of the northwest of what is now Canada, as well as Washington, Oregon, and northern California. We also consider tribes of the region between the Rocky Mountains and the Sierra and Cascade ranges. The tribes of the Northwest were distinctive for the special influence of Asian traits, including the use of conical hats. They usually lived fairly easily because good fishing was readily available, along with lumber for simple building. They produced totem poles with fabulous faces, and their most distinctive ritual, the ceremonial feast known as the potlatch, has fascinated anthropologists.

For the potlatch, people invited others to a great feast. Status derived from being able to provide lavishly for one's guests, and also from knowing precisely how to arrange such guests. Tribes of the Northwest tended to value status highly—knowing the rankings of many people and the rituals handed down for the conduct of the potlatch marked one as shrewd, on top of things, capable of leadership.

Behind the potlatch meal lay the conviction that the spiritual powers running the world needed to be embodied in flesh, and that they gave themselves through the animals that provided the tribe's food. It was important not to hoard these spiritual powers; unless they were circulating freely throughout the group, the group was in trouble. Selfishness, possessiveness, and a lack of generosity were major social and spiritual failings. Grievances and disorders were thought to come from an unfair distribution of material resources. The more people ensured that all members of the tribe participated fully in the bounty of the earth, the more that happiness and prosperity would flower. The potlatch served to

> maintain social equilibrium, consolidate chiefly power over common-
> ers, provide for the orderly transfer of wealth and power, provide a
> measure of group identity and solidarity, redistribute surplus wealth
> and level economic imbalances, provide outlets for competition with-
> out recourse to violence, and provide an occasion for aesthetic
> expression and entertainment. . . . [S]ince in Northwest Coast phi-
> losophy all status, power, and wealth are considered to be a gift from
> the beneficent supernatural beings who provide the materials that
> human beings need to survive, the potlatch is inherently a religious
> institution, fundamentally endowed with a sacramental quality.[9]

The raven is an important figure in Northwest mythology, serving as the leading culture hero and trickster. A culture hero brings to a tribe important features of its traditional way of life—for example, use of fire, ways of fishing, methods for making pots or building houses. A trickster is a canny, impulsive being whose antics amuse the people and yet also teach them lessons, both positive and negative, in how to survive.

In one story about the raven, he was wearing an orange feather. The wife of a fisherman saw him, admired his feather, and asked where she could get one. Raven promised to take her husband to an island nearby, where there were robins. When he and the fisherman went to the island, Raven secretly changed old pieces of wood into birds and made them fly to the interior. While the husband went after the birds, Raven changed himself to look just like the husband and returned to where the man lived. He went to the man's favorite pond, hauled out the best fish, and made himself a wonderful meal. The wife thought nothing of it, because she assumed that her husband had come home hungry. The fisherman returned grumpy, because the orange feathers he had collected on the island soon turned back into old pieces of wood. When he learned that Raven had eaten his best fish, he fell on him, knocked him senseless, and

---

[9] Stanley Walens, "Potlatch," in *The Encyclopedia of Religion*, 11: 465.

threw him into the water, where Raven was swallowed by a huge fish. When he revived, Raven tormented the fish until it swam to shore. There a fisherman caught it and cut it open. Raven jumped out, unharmed and free to pursue further adventures.[10]

This tale suggests several lessons. First, it may be dangerous to admire the possessions of others. Second, what seems beautiful may really be, or soon become, old, commonplace, even ugly. Third, it is necessary always to keep one's wits sharp. The fisherman was too trusting, and so was his wife. Raven thrived by trickery, and so may any human being. Fourth, trickery may be found out and the tricky person thrashed. Fifth, even punishment is not likely to do in a truly shrewd person. People who keep their wits about them can escape from difficult circumstances and be free to scheme another day. Sixth, natural creatures like the Raven may simply be perverse.

The idea of creating the earth from the bottom of the primeval waters was a common notion among oral peoples. The Maidu of northern California traditionally told a story of creation featuring a heavenly being called earth-initiate. He shone so brightly that no one could look upon his face. The sun was his sister, and he made both the earth and the stars. The earth was all watery. When the turtle grew tired of having to swim endlessly, of having no place to rest, he begged earth-initiate for some dry land. Earth-initiate agreed to let the turtle dive to the bottom of the sea. The turtle was gone six years, connected to the surface only by a rope tied around his leg. Eventually he brought back a tiny bit of mud, jammed under his nails. Earth-initiate rolled this mud into a little ball, which then grew into the great ball of the earth.[11]

The story is instructive on several scores. First, our earth comes from heaven, by the approval and work of beings above. Second, these beings cooperate with animals. Here the turtle is the designated helper. In other versions another aquatic animal, or even a bird, dives under the waters. Third, the preponderance of water over earth may reflect a traditional view of consciousness: What appears in the mind clear and solid is only a fraction of human awareness. Most of what we know and are lies in our depths.

For some natives of the intermountain region, spirit-quests were important. Winter was set aside for ritual activity, much of which was a series of spirit-dances. At the time of puberty, both boys and girls could seek guiding spirits. If they gained them, they could enter religious societies that sponsored dances, festivals, and the chance to deepen one's appreciation of the spiritual life. To help children gain a spiritual helper, adults would instruct them to fast, bathe in cold streams, endure

---

[10] See Cottie Burland et al., *Mythology of the Americas* (New York: Hamlyn, 1970), 39.

[11] See Allen A. Macfarlan, ed., *American Indian Legends* (New York: Heritage Press, 1968), 3.

solitude, and afflict their bodies in other ways. Those seeking a vision needed to deny their carnal appetites and sharpen their spiritual hunger. Often, if the young person had been diligent, the spiritual helper would appear in a dream. Usually it took the form of an animal and stayed with the young person for the rest of his or her life. Typically, the spiritual helper imparted a distinctive song and dance, which became the person's religious signature. At the winter festivals members of the intermountain tribes would sing their songs and dance their dances, weaving a kind of spiritual tapestry. The individual songs rang changes on general convictions about the goodness of creation, the need to be virtuous, the beauties of the surrounding land. Shamans would help young people put their visions to rest, so that at maturity the power of the guiding spirit might burst forth again, to help them carry adult responsibilities.

Myths and rituals like these remind us that Native Americans possessed a dramatic consciousness. Their imaginations were filled with sights and sounds tied to spiritual forces thought to be guiding their lives. They sought to experience this guidance, by singing and dancing their way to contact with their spiritual helpers. Though they could also pursue such helpers in solitude, the emphasis placed by traditional peoples on the community stimulated them to share their visions and faith. The visions of one became part of the legacy of all. The power that one received supported another's quest for further power, wisdom, the ability to find the world beautiful and significant.

Natives of the Southwest

Many of the tribes that lived in southern California, Baja California in Mexico, Arizona, New Mexico, and southern Colorado practiced agriculture. Probably the Pueblo peoples of New Mexico have been the most studied. The Hopi, a Pueblo people, are famous for their involved rituals, many of which have featured masked dancers called kachinas. Typically, the kachinas perform from January through July, in more than 300 different masks and spirits. While dancing, the person becomes the kachina. Children grow up thinking that the kachinas are incarnate spirits, and even adults reject the idea that human beings merely impersonate the spirits. Something more intimate and profound is involved. By way of the dances the spirits that represent the most significant forces in Hopi life—forces of fertility, healing, and sustenance, as well as challenge—come into the people's midst. Plant and animal spirits important to the tribe dance and sing, reminding the tribe of what they are immersed in, what their survival entails. The kachinas may be friendly, approachable, but they still convey to traditional Hopi something awesome.

From January to March the kachina dances tend to take place at night, in the kivas, or underground dwellings, that represent the place where the world originated, where one can feel close to the power of creation. From April to July the kachinas usually appear during the day in the village square. Toward the end of the kachina season unmasked clowns may accompany the masked dancers. Their satiric commentary links the dances to the current state of the tribe, holding a mirror up to those who need to mend their ways.

Two highlights of the kachina season are a bean festival, which occurs in February, and a homegoing ceremony for the kachinas in July. The bean festival comes at the time of planting, when the importance of beans for the sustenance of the tribe is especially clear. At the end of the kachina season, the spirits depart from the tribe, returning to their homes in the mountains. It is important to send them on their way full of the prayers and thanks of the Hopi people.[12]

As the ritual dances and songs developed and took on more meaning, the yearly festivals would become miniatures of the entire tribal culture. Everything essential for the survival and well-being of the people was represented. The spirits crucial to tribal life came into view to be both admired and feared. The social relations of the community were brought forth for repair. Children were instructed in the ways of their culture, as the old were strengthened for death by seeing how the present life bore on the afterlife. Men and women could learn the tasks and obligations of their sex. The main occupations—growing beans and corn, weaving blankets, making pots, caring for children, dealing with enemies, warding off the misfortunes of sickness, drought, and infertility—took their places. Indeed, the tribe exercised forms of religion, psychotherapy, entertainment, and political renewal: the entire local culture was reaffirmed, renewed, and healed for another year.

The Navaho, who probably came into the Southwest from the Plains shortly before the advent of the whites, were as ritualistic as the Hopi. As they were more concerned about witchcraft, however, their ceremonies focused more on combating powers of evil. Clyde Kluckhohn, a leading anthropologist of the past generation, recounts a piece of Navaho gossip about witches:

> When witch people get together, they talk about things. One person will say to another man, 'When I was out there at the people, one man got mad at me or one woman. And what I want to do about that man or woman. I want to kill that man.' One reason the other witches will be glad to kill this man is after they kill him they'll make more medicine, fresh medicine. When they kill him they go out and get him and bring him inside to this hogan

---

[12] See Peter Whitely, "North American Indians: Indians of the Southwest," in *The Encyclopedia of Religion*, 10: 519–521.

[house]. For a man can be made into that medicine. If they kill a woman, a good woman, they'll bring her down here inside the hogan and one man can have intercourse with her. Maybe two, maybe three, maybe all of them can have intercourse with her. Put a little pot or something underneath her and catch the stuff. Make medicine out of that too.[13]

In this context, "medicine" is something evil. In most other contexts, Native North Americans use medicine to connote sources of healing. Witches are people of spiritual power bent on evil. They traffic in murder, sexual abuse, and everything else from the darker recesses of the Navaho imagination. Gossip about witches may well be a safety valve, a way for Navaho to externalize their fears of horrible things and come to grips with them.

Because Navaho culture thinks of sickness as holistic, psychosomatic, it tries to effect healing through singing, dancing, the ministrations of shamanic healers, and sandpaintings. The paintings represent the spiritual condition of the person, which can point to the current state of nature or the tribe. Witches, too, had their rituals, their wicked paintings, their evil medicine. Such medicine would come from and deal with death, pollution, illness, abuse. The battle for the Navaho psyche has been a battle between good medicine and bad, spiritual people who heal and spiritual people bent on causing harm. Because nature itself housed evil as well as good, this was a crucial battle.

In a more positive vein, Navaho songs to bless a hogan, like the one whose words follow, illustrate the connection made between human flourishing and natural beauty:

Far in the east far below there a house was made; delightful house. God of Dawn there his house was made; delightful house. The dawn there his house was made; delightful house. White corn there its house was made; delightful house. Soft possessions for them a house was made; delightful house. Corn pollen for it a house was made; delightful house. The ancients made their presence delightful; delightful house. Before me may it be delightful; behind me may it be delightful; around me may it be delightful; below me may it be delightful; above me may it be delightful; all may it be delightful.[14]

The song brings together most of the major concerns of a traditional people's way of life: a place to live, the natural elements, food, the ancients, all the directions. Only the animals are missing, and other songs, or other parts of this song, may well include them. To have "a house made of dawn"—of light, possibility, splendor—would be to have

---

[13] Clyde Kluckhohn, *Navaho Witchcraft* (Boston: Beacon Press, 1967/1944), 133–134.

[14] Sam D. Gill, *Native American Traditions* (Belmont, CA: Wadsworth, 1983), 28.

the most blessed of human lives,[15] to celebrate the goodness of creation. The hogan is a miniature of the world. Within it should occur relations forged in honesty and love. Around it should occur delight on every side, beauty, the song of the entire world.

Tribes in the Southwest had special interests and special problems. Because drought threatened their farming they were especially concerned with rain. Their religion focused relatively little on the spirits of game, concerning itself more with corn and beans. Their villages were larger and more longstanding than those of migratory peoples, producing more elaborate social relations. Southwest tribal culture made a larger place for priests and religious societies because it was more complex, more stable, better positioned to develop and celebrate extended rituals. Indeed, it seems that rituals were at times the people's main business, with farming and other practical affairs secondary.

Nature and Society

Of the four dimensions basic to any worldview—nature, society, self, and divinity—nature and society are well represented in Native North American mythology and ritual, with nature the more prominent. Nature is not seen as an inert, impersonal, unfeeling other, as brute matter. On the contrary, it is the matrix, the mother, the holy living environment.

The holiness of nature has stemmed from its divinity. The gods or powerful spirits stirred nature and directed it. The heavens above, the earth below, the winged creatures, the four-legged creatures, the fish— all moved because they were inspirited. To move, or simply to *be*, in a significant manner was to be filled with a spiritual presence. The natural world was abuzz with spiritual powers. Dawn was a holy presence for the Navaho, as for the Pueblo peoples of the Southwest. To rise early in the morning, climb to the roof of one's pueblo, and greet the sun was to participate in a holy process. What could be more significant than the rising of the sun, the great power responsible for all light and warmth? What could give greater dignity to human beings than helping the sun on his way, through prayers of praise and petition?

In his autobiography, the psychologist Carl Gustav Jung recounts an interview he had with an elderly Pueblo Indian who used to greet the sun this way. They were in Taos, New Mexico, and Jung was slowly learning how to discern what Native Americans' religious ideas meant to them:

> Direct questioning led to nothing. When, therefore, I wanted to know about essential matters, I made tentative remarks and observed my interlocutor's expression . . . If I had hit on something

---

[15] See N. Scott Momaday, *House Made of Dawn* (New York: Harper & Row, 1977).

essential, he remained silent or gave an evasive reply, but with all the signs of profound emotions; frequently tears would fill his eyes. Their religious conceptions are not theories to them (which, indeed, would have to be very curious theories to evoke tears from a man), but facts, as important and moving as the corresponding external realities.

As I sat with Ochwiay Biano on the roof, the blazing sun rising higher and higher, he said, pointing to the sun, "Is not he who moves there our father? How can anyone say differently? How can there be another god? Nothing can be without the sun." His excitement, which was already perceptible, mounted still higher; he struggled for words, and exclaimed at last, "What would a man do alone in the mountains? He cannot even build his fire without him."

I asked him whether he did not think the sun might be a fiery ball shaped by an invisible god. My question did not even arouse astonishment, let alone anger. Obviously it touched nothing within him; he did not think my question stupid. It merely left him cold. I had the feeling that I had come upon an insurmountable wall. His only reply was, "The sun is God. Everyone can see that."[16]

For the Native North American, divinity—the sacred, the most truly real—manifested itself in nature. Nature was more than simply itself, as the sun was more than just a star giving light and warmth to the earth.

Native Americans were mystified, intrigued, overwhelmed, profoundly involved in the primordial fact that the world exists, and is in so rich a way. Naturally, they were not profoundly involved all the time, or without concern for mundane, even unworthy desires, preoccupations, expenditures of energy. But it is clear that contemplation of the mysteries of natural existence was the soul of traditional Native North American culture.

We have noted the willingness of Native Americans to care for the welfare of their fellow tribal members. Lame Deer's vision made him a healer, a servant of the needs of his fellow human beings. Sioux sun dancers sacrificed themselves for the well-being of the Sioux nation. The various secret societies found in many tribes did not war against this notion. Their function, more often than not, was to help ordinary tribal members share in the tribal lore and the wisdom that was peculiar to the shaman. The secret societies tended to democratize shamanic wisdom, often with the agreement of shamans themselves. Secret societies also served to continue the initiation that most tribes practiced at the time of puberty. Passing from childhood to adulthood required stepping into the mysteries of sexuality, procreation, death, and service to the holy powers controlling human destiny.

---

[16] C. G. Jung, *Memories, Dreams, Reflections* (New York: Vintage, 1961), 250–251.

Ake Hultkrantz, a scholar of Native American religions, speaks of secret societies as "collective transformations of the institution of the medicine man."

> The tribal initiation rites, the men's societies, and the rites of intro-
> duction to the tribe in one place correspond to initiation rites to
> the secret society in another. Data from the Northwest Coast and
> the Great Lakes prove that members of the societies *de facto* had the
> capacity and functions of medicine men. . . . [P]uberty rites have
> provided a pattern for forms of initiation, the men's societies (wher-
> ever they have existed) have encouraged tendencies toward seclu-
> sion and secrecy, and the institution of the medicine man has con-
> tributed by rendering purpose and force to the societies.[17]

Native North American peoples wanted to penetrate more deeply the mysteries of nature that their religious myths and rituals laid before them. Through such key tasks as healing, education, and male bonding, smaller groups specified the tribe's general desire to win the favor of the holy powers running the cosmos and to appreciate their beauty. The secret societies furthered engagements with the sacred, the holy.

The Self and Divinity

The Native North American concept of self is probably clearest in the shamans, who stand out as the most compelling figures in Native North American societies and who possessed great individual power. In other areas of tribal life, the self's prominence varied. In hunting, where personal skill was paramount, the individual was nearly as important as the tribe. The more complicated society became, the less power the individual had over the group. Although agriculture increased tribal wealth and tended to allow people to specialize, the development of pottery, weaving, and rituals stayed under community control so that the individual tended to lose clout. Larger Native American groups created significant priesthoods, as we see in the chapter on Central and South American tribes. These priesthoods usually had political, if not military, influence and were the centers of learning. A few priest-kings stand out in the historical record, but as religious cultures became more organized the individual tended to become submerged in tradition, ceremony, and concern for the institutional priesthood (the group holding power). Similarly, regarding the relations between individual warriors and larger or smaller armies, the more complex the military structure, the less likely was it to be individualistic.

---

[17] Ake Hultkrantz, *The Religions of the American Indians* (Berkeley: University of California Press, 1979), 118, 119.

For the Shaman, singing was the way to supreme individuation. People most became themselves when they were filled with their songs, could move through their songs like birds through the air. A song was a passport to the center of the self. Inasmuch as one's song was a gift from a spiritual helper, and a reminder of one's initiatory vision, it was both a link with the supernatural world and an epitome of the experience in which one first glimpsed one's mature self.

Some tribes of the far north thought that the shaman's song pointed the way to the center of all holiness:

> Song stands at the intimate center of the cosmos of the individual. At that moment when the shaman song emerges, when the sacred breath rises up from the depths of the heart, the center is found, and the source of all that is divine has been tapped.

> On the Alaskan island called Little Diomede, Knud Rasmussen [a Danish explorer of the Arctic] encountered an old woman living among the shreds of her life in a cold, dark cave. A diviner, she had seen many seasons come and go and many lives pass as the seasons do. She spoke to the Greenlander of her own life and imminent passing. Her final words to him concerned the genesis of song. With eloquent and profound insight, she described the source of the sacred sounds that are the most important of the shaman's voices, those voices that awaken during threshold experiences: "For our forefathers believed that the songs were born in stillness while all endeavored to think of nothing but beautiful things. Then they take shape in the minds of men and rise up like bubbles from the depths of the sea, bubbles seeking air in order to burst. This is how sacred songs are made."[18]

Shamans use songs as one of several ways to manipulate their consciousness. A song partakes of the circulation of the breath, which many spiritual explorers have recognized as a crucial link between thought and sensation, spirit and body.

Many shamans learned to sing in eerie, moving tones. They learned to narrate their journeys, placate the gods, plead for the spirits of the dead or for the sick. They became artists, their voices their chief instruments. As they matured, and their selves became bound to their shamanic work, they could reach the point where they sang and went into trance as a spiritual necessity. Even when there was no one to heal, no crisis to solve, they felt compelled to "work." Their nervous systems had become accustomed to singing, shamanizing. Without regular travel in the spiritual world, they felt out of sorts, unwell. Many saints in theistic traditions have reported similar feelings about prayer. Without regular immersion in and contemplation of the divinity at the center of their lives, their sense of well-being was impaired.

---

[18] Joan Halifax, *Shamanic Voices* (New York: E. P. Dutton, 1979), 30.

Turning to divinity, we find that Plains Indians such as the Pawnee offer a good example of the roster of gods that many Native North Americans honored.

> The Pawnee elaborated a series of myths that described the creation of the world, the origin of humans and the power of the gods. The Pawnee believed that Tirawa, the supreme being, was married to the Vault of Heaven, and both reigned somewhere in the heavens in a place beyond the clouds. Yet they were purely spiritual beings and took no earthly shape. Tirawa sent his commands to humans through a number of lesser gods and messengers who manifested themselves to the Pawnee. Next in importance to Tirawa and his wife was Teuperika ("evening star"), who was personified as a young maiden. Evening Star was keeper of a garden in the west that was the source of all food. She had four assistants, Wind, Cloud, Lightning, and Thunder. She married Oprikata ("morning star"), and from them was born the first human being on earth. Morning Star was perceived as a strong warrior who drove the rest of the stars before him.[19]

Human beings were the offspring of divine forces, in this case of the evening and morning stars. Behind the imagery lay the intuition that human beings could not explain themselves, and also the desire to give men and women a sacred origin. Such a sacred origin meant that human beings could call upon the divine forces. Even when the greatest divinity responsible for the world seemed remote, one could deal with delegated gods or goddesses. The result was a worldview in which anything could become a presence of the divine. Rock, tree, bird, flower, fish, wolf—the divine could transmit its message or power through any of them. Few Native North Americans deified any human figure. Holy as a shaman or priest might become, he or she was not a god. But the power by which the shaman healed or divined came from the holy spirits, the gods. To be successful, the shaman or priest had to be connected with heaven or the earth. By extension, a person's life required for its flourishing connection with the holy powers. A man or woman would find fulfillment only through communion with the holy, the truly ultimate reality.

Study Questions

1. Explain the centrality of visions and ceremonies in traditional Native North American religions.
2. Of what significance was the land to traditional Native Americans of the Far North?

---

[19]William K. Powers, "North American Indians: Indians of the Plains," *The Encyclopedia of Religion*, 10: 494.

3. How did Eastern Woodlands Indians connect warfare with the possibility of spiritual blessings?
4. Explain the symbolism of the feathered wand in the Hako ceremony of the Central Plains.
5. In what ways did the potlatch represent much of religious culture in the Northwest?
6. What did the Hopi believe about the kachinas?
7. What was the basis for Navaho ideas about witchcraft?
8. Describe the place of the sun in the world of the Pueblos.
9. How did the shaman's song become the center of his or her personality?

CHAPTER 3

Natives of Central and South America

Overview

Although the natives of what is now called Latin America developed hieroglyphic writing, their roots and most of their people remained oral. The largest native civilizations occurred in what is now Mexico and the Andes of South America. A number of societies large enough to be called empires developed in Central America. The Olmecs, Toltecs, Aztecs, Mayas and other peoples produced significant cultures. In the Andes the great culture was that of the Inca. Both the Aztecs and the Inca were in full sway when Spanish conquerors arrived early in the sixteenth century. Since that time, Native Latin American religion has come under the influence of Christianity.

Nowadays it is customary to speak of Latin America as Christian (traditionally Roman Catholic, but increasingly also Protestant). Nonetheless, in remote areas native pre-Christian ways remain strong, and even in areas where Christian predominance seems clear, native traditions are influential. Indeed, folk Christianity has fascinated many scholars, leading to interesting studies of such phenomena as Guadalupism, the devotions developed in response to the visionary appearances of the Virgin of Guadalupe, outside Mexico City. Latin American Christianity clearly owes a debt to Iberian (Spanish and Portuguese) Christianity, yet it has distinctive features, owing largely to native Central or South American traditions.

Consider, for example, the following excerpt from an ethnological sketch of the life of a typical modern-day Mexican peasant named Juan:

One night I dreamed that an uncle and aunt of mine came to visit me. They gave me two horses to take care of, also some hay to feed them. Later I found out what the dream meant: my uncle was San Juan, my aunt was the Virgin of the Rosary, and the two horses belonged to the priest. It meant I was going to receive another duty, because afterwards I was made a sacristan. The sacristans take care of the church, and their duty lasts their whole life. I've served my village in many ways, and they keep on giving me duties. I was alferez [representative] of the Virgin of the Rosary, but I asked for that duty myself. The mayordomos and alferez can sell liquor, and that makes up for what they spend during the fiesta.[1]

The churches that need sacristans and the saints who need representatives to protect their interests and advance their cult obviously come from Christianity. But the speaker's tendency to find his future revealed in dreams probably comes from Native American culture. Juan seems to identify with San Juan. Names are important in Native American thought. The designation that one carries says much about one's character. In more remote parts of Latin America, where Christian influence is weaker, shamans continue to cast *mites* (divination beans) to determine what name a new infant should receive. They may also study astrological charts, believing that the time when the child was born holds the key to its fate. Even though a peasant like Juan may know little about the history of his people prior to the coming of the whites—and though his own bloodline may be a mixture of native and white contributions—old, pre-Christian instincts like trusting in dreams to disclose the future can continue to guide him through life.

Human beings have been in Central and South America for at least 10,000 years. Whether they emigrated south from upper North America, or arrived on the west coast from southern Asia by boat (with no dependence on the people who supposedly began colonizing North America by crossing the Bering Strait), they appear to be of the same parent stock as Native North Americans. The major cultural differences that exist between the two continents probably derive from differences in habitat—the need to respond to different ecological niches. Sufficient time has elapsed to explain considerable cultural evolution.

Central America has proven to be a fertile field for archaeological exploration. For instance, at the time of the white conquest there were more than 100 Mayan ceremonial centers, each offering a treasure trove of artifacts, some of which dated to at least the third century B.C.E. The remains found at Tikal, in the central region of classical Mayan influence, suggest that this ceremonial center extended for about one square

[1] Richard Pozas, *Juan the Chamula* (Berkeley: University of California Press, 1962), 106.

mile and housed a population of about 10,000 people. There were at least six stepped pyramids, or temples, the largest standing almost 230 feet high. Remains found in areas dominated by the Olmecs, the first people in the line that led to the Aztecs, date to at least the ninth century B.C.E., probably to several centuries earlier. Thus, for nearly 2,500 years Central Americans had a well-developed culture, with fairly elaborate temple grounds and, presumably, fairly elaborate religious rituals. These rituals are one of our main interests.

In dealing with South American traditions, we find that, apart from the high cultures developed in the Andes, much of the Native religious history pivots on shamans, experts in ecstatic healing. The basic economy was that of hunters and gatherers, although in numerous areas there was also farming. But populations tended to be small in such areas as the Amazonian forests, the Gran Chaco, Patagonia, and the southernmost region now known as Tierra del Fuego. Thus, some of the patterns that we saw among hunters and gatherers of North America reappear, though naturally each tribe and area has had its own distinctive characteristics.

Natural beauty has been a powerful force in the cultures of Latin America, as it has for Native North Americans. Florinda Donner, an anthropologist who worked with the Yanomama Indians of southern Venezuela and northern Brazil, a tribe she found almost untouched by white influence, describes the impact of natural beauty she felt in the company of natives:

> We reached the top of a plateau eroded by winds and rains, a relic from another age. Below, the forest was still asleep under a blanket of fog. A mysterious, pathless world whose vastness one could never guess from the outside. We sat on the ground and silently waited for the sun to rise. An overwhelming sense of awe brought me to my feet as the sky in the east glowed red and purple along the horizon. The clouds, obedient to the wind, opened to let the rising disk through. . . . The sun had lifted the blanket of fog. The river shone like a golden snake cutting through the greenness until it lost itself in an immensity of space that seemed to be part of another world. I wanted to speak, to cry out loud, but I had no words with which to express my emotions. Looking at Ritimi and Etewa, I knew they understood how deeply I felt. I held out my arms as if to embrace this marvelous border of forest and sky. I felt I was at the edge of time and space. I could hear the vibrations of the light, the whispering of trees, the cries of distant birds carried by the wind.[2]

Donner's experience must have been different from that of Ritimi and Etewa. Yet, cutting across cultural divides, this beauty united them in

---

[2] Florinda Donner, *Shabono* (New York: Delacorte, 1982), 162–163.

their sense of common humanity. Regardless of their differences as white and brown, European and Native American, they shared a capacity to be awed by the beauty of the world, the sacred splendor of sky, wind, forest, and sun.

Olmec Religion

Between 1,200 and 600 B.C.E., the Olmec people occupied the tropical lowlands of southern Mexico, in what are now the states of Veracruz and Tabasco. They built villages, grew corn, and produced pottery. What distinguished them from their neighbors, however, was their development of larger social units and extensive cultic sites. To build their impressive temples, they created a distinctive architecture. They also became outstanding sculptors, working in stone and jade to create both monumental pieces of art and exquisite smaller pieces.

> The Olmecs commemorated rulers in their art, but it was basically religious in content, being focused upon a wide variety of supernaturals which combined features of the animal world with those of humans, blending into each other in bewildering complexity. Only in recent years have we come to realize that the Olmec had an extensive pantheon, for it used to be thought that their only god was the characteristic "were-jaguar," which combined the features of a snarling jaguar with those of a bawling infant.
>
> Thanks to the chance discovery in 1965 of a large greenstone figure at Las Limas, Veracruz, we can now appreciate that there were many Olmec gods, each with its own attributes, although these were freely exchanged with those of other supernaturals. The Las Limas figure depicts a young man or adolescent seated tailor-fashion, holding the familiar were-jaguar infant in his arms; four other deities, all with the mysterious cleft heads typical of Olmec gods, are incised on his shoulder and knees.[3]

The identification between human beings and jaguars that we see beginning with the Olmecs continues to appear in the later great Central American cultures, such as that of the Toltecs, the predecessors of the Aztecs. Eventually Quetzalcoatl, the feathered serpent, became the leading religious figure of Mexico, but the following sketch of how ancient Mexican religion may have evolved suggests the ongoing impact of the Olmec:

> Evidently the jaguar held primacy among the Olmecs. . . . [H]e symbolized terror and the mystery of the jungle, of life, of the other

---

[3] Michael Coe, Dean Snow, and Elizabeth Benson, *Atlas of Ancient America* (New York: Facts on File, 1986), 96.

world. He was imbued with all forms: that of a deified animal, at times magnificently sculptured in jade or stone; at times he is seen complete, or only his face is stylized in masks; at other times he is a humanized jaguar, a man-jaguar, or a child-jaguar. Even today many popular legends related to the jaguar theme are common. . . . Frequently we are not dealing with a simple jaguar, but with a monstrous jaguar far removed from a realistic representation. Elements characteristic of man and of other animals have been added, mainly those of a bird and a serpent. Thus the jaguar is likely to have feathers over his eyes instead of eyebrows. This association of a jaguar with feathers, that is, with a bird, is important furthermore because it is possibly the origin of the great god who also brings together a bird with another animal: Quetzalcoatl, the feathered serpent. By then a bird—a quetzal or eagle—was to take the place of the lowland jaguar in the iconography of the high plateau of Mexico.[4]

The persistence of artistic themes from Olmec to Aztec times argues that even the classical Mesoamerican religious cultures remained close to the vivid, oral world that sponsored the early fascination with the jaguar. A were-jaguar (human-jaguar) is a dramatic expression of the feeling, common among oral, hunting peoples, that human beings and animals are locked together inseparably. The jaguar fascinated prehistoric hunters of the Central American jungles, because it stood for death, power, animal vitality. Hunters, like jaguars, could inflict death; they too had to be silent, swift, resourceful. To merge with the jaguar in spirit was to gain some of its strengths. Even more, it was to enter into the mysteries of creation. The beauty and power of the jaguar, like that of the shark, or the dangerous allure of the alligator, or the horrible yet graceful work of the harpy eagle, brought into human beings' midst the mysterious, unintelligible fact that the natural world was organized so that life should feed upon life, so that death should permeate even the most lush system of fauna and flora. Religion began in wonder at this fact.

The oral character of Olmec and much subsequent Mexican religious culture allowed an imaginative freedom to play with the possible permutations of the sacred power responsible for the world. No texts determined what the jaguar had meant in the past and would continue to mean in the present. Certainly, sacred art, iconography, has a stabilizing, conservative effect, but it does not fix the conceptual mind as written texts do.

Images lead to dramatic possibilities in oral cultures. Admittedly, the texts of written cultures also invite imagination. Literature stands or falls by the degree to which it stimulates people to imagine. But this stimulus

---

[4] Ignacio Bernal, *The Olmec World* (Berkeley: University of California Press, 1969), 99.

is more abstract than that which prompts the shaman to *become*, in trance, the jaguar, right down to its snarl and leap. The reader wants to observe the jaguar, to contemplate it safely at a distance; it is another matter to seek to have the jaguar take over one's consciousness, to oust human identity and establish jaguarhood.

Mayan Religion

The high point of Mayan civilization was the period 300–900 C.E., when a rich culture flourished in the Peten lowlands of northern Guatemala. Although Christianity has influenced modern Mayans, many of the ideas developed in the classical, pre-Christian era continue to shape people of Mayan extraction. The classical Mayans organized their territory into city-states, the centers of which were ceremonial precincts. There they built the pyramids for which they are famous and other huge monuments. They cultivated maize, but also practiced a swidden (cut-and-burn) agriculture. By 800 C.E. they probably had reached a population of about two million. More than three million of their descendants now live in the Yucatan Peninsula, the highlands of Guatemala, and the state of Chiapas, Mexico.

The consuming interest of the classical Mayans was the religious calendar. Mayan priests produced some remarkably sophisticated astronomical calculations under the belief that their fate was tied up with the positions of the planets and stars.

> [Their] concern with the passage of time led the Maya to chart the motions and phases of the sun, moon, Venus, and various constellations. By calculating the duration of different celestial cycles in terms of whole-day units (e.g., 149 lunations = 4,400 days), Classic Maya astronomers were able to compute lunar periods, the length of the solar year, and the revolutions of Venus, all to within minutes of their modern values. These calculations were greatly facilitated by the invention of a system of place-value arithmetic, an achievement that the Maya share only with the ancient Mesopotamians. . . . The coalescence in Maya thought of time, astronomy, mathematics, and writing finds expression in Itzamna, the principal deity of the Classic Maya: he was alternatively the creator god, the sun, and the first priest who invented writing and books.[5]

From oral beginnings, the Mayans moved to literacy of a hieroglyphic sort because they were desperate to know the structures of time. For rea-

---

[5] John H. Watanabe, "Maya Religion," in *The Encyclopedia of Religion*, ed. Mircea Eliade (New York: Macmillan, 1987), 9: 298.

sons not clear to us, they became convinced that the motions of the celestial bodies were the key to the meaning of their own existence. They needed ways to represent the calculations they made of the passage of the sun and other heavenly bodies, which led them to both numerical and pictorial abstractions. In all this strenuous calculation they were moved by the instinct, common to peoples shaped by the cosmological myth that the world is a single living entity, that what goes on above, in the heavens, is the archetype for what goes on below, on earth.

Space and time were traced by the movement of the sun across the heavens. The sun was the creator, and the movement of the sun was the dynamic source of creation. The spatial axis of Mayan thought ran from east to west. East was represented by the color red, west by the color black (the rising and setting of the sun). North and south were represented by white and yellow. The cosmic pillar (the first tree, representing vegetative creation), was blue-green. These colors could be manipulated to create another shorthand system for referring to the space that conditioned time. When the sun passed from sight to move through the underworld, it took on the guise of the jaguar. The god Itzamna, who could stand for the sun, was represented by a two-headed reptile, the celestial monster, who encircled the plane of the earth's surface.

These and many other complicated symbols suggest what happens when an oral people moves from commonsense images of the heavens to protoscience. As they calculate positions and planes, oral peoples seldom lose their imaginative immersion in the forces they are trying to comprehend. Any move to abstraction, for instance through mathematical developments, is balanced by a retention of vivid images, such as those of the reptilian god or the sun-as-jaguar. It is useful to specify the movements of the celestial bodies, and so calculate how time unfolded in the past and can be expected to proceed in the future, but the drama of the situation requires that people continue to imagine the forces ruling their lives as possessing a combination of animal and human attributes.

The priestly class that specialized in calculations and iconography such as this could develop because agricultural advances had provided enough prosperity to support a nonproductive group. Inasmuch as they generated and controlled sacred information, the priests had great power. They were in league with the Mayan kings, who established hereditary dynasties. Deceased rulers turned into gods, and the major ceremonial centers have provided artifacts suggesting that significant cults grew up around deceased rulers. Such an honoring of eminent ancestors and rulers probably expresses another facet of the Mayan concern with time. The deceased ancestors were once-palpable presences of time. In venerating them, Mayans could make the past contemporary. They could gain some small control over time. The terror of time is that it is always slipping away. Surveying time past and imagining time future enables human beings to gain a small release from the prison of time.

Though their bodies are sure to die, perhaps their spirits can outwit death, transcend the current moment, move back and forth through time.

The *Popul Vuh*, a Mayan text sometimes called the *Book of Counsel*, represents a crystallization of Mayan traditions after the arrival of whites and the introduction of a Romanized alphabet. Although scholars discern some influence on the *Popul Vuh* of Christian ideas, as well as of Central American peoples like the Toltecs, who flourished after the golden age of Mayan civilization, it is generally agreed that the text is a valuable source of information about traditional Mayan beliefs. In other words, the origins of the images that we find in this written text may well lie in preliterate days; the images continue to play in the minds of present-day peasants of Mayan extraction, some of whom are barely literate.

The following is a description of the time of creation contained in the *Popul Vuh*:

> Truly it was yet quiet, truly it was yet stilled. It was quiet. Truly it was calm. Truly it was solitary and it was also still empty, the womb of heaven. These are truly then the first words, the first utterances. There was not one person yet, one animal, deer, bird, fish, crab, tree, rock, hole, canyon, meadow or forest. All by itself the sky existed. The face of the earth was not yet visible. All by itself the sea lay dammed, and the womb of heaven, everything. There was nothing whatever, silenced or at rest. Each thing was made silent, each thing was made calm, was made invisible, was made to rest in heaven. There was not, then, anything in fact that was standing there. Only the pooled water, only the flat sea.[6]

Eventually Quetzalcoatl, the plumed serpent, works with Majesty, another heavenly personage, to arrange the world. But the silent, empty origins of the cosmos, the primacy of nothingness, are striking. Did the Mayans' longstanding concern with the heavens bring home the emptiness of celestial space, the predominance of darkness over light? Or were they projecting a psychological sensitivity—human awareness, "light," comes out of the darkness of ignorance and the subconscious—onto a conception of creation? The human sense of form, definition, which allows the mind to think it comprehends and therefore can control, comes after immersion in the formless, the chaotic, which overwhelms consciousness and makes comprehension impossible.

The *Popul Vuh* pictures the formation of the world as an act that engaged Majesty and the Feathered Serpent emotionally. Moved to create by good feelings, they acted from the heart: "Then they thought; then they pondered. Then they found themselves. They assembled their

---

[6] Miguel Leon-Portilla, ed., *Native Mesoamerican Spirituality* (New York: Paulist Press, 1980), 103–104.

words, their thoughts. Then they gave birth, then they heartened themselves. Then they caused to be created, and they bore men. Then they thought about the birth, the creation of trees and shrubs, and the birth of life and humanity in the obscurity, in the nighttime, through him who is the Heart of Heaven, One Leg, by name."[7] One Leg refers to lightning; thus, the source of creation is a bolt of power, light, and energy.

Aztec Religion

The Aztecs were the predominant Central American power at the time of white, Christian conquest in the sixteenth century. Their culture owed more to the Olmecs and the Toltecs than to the Mayans, but the Mayans had influenced all Central American peoples, as those peoples in turn had influenced the Mayans. The Aztecs, somewhat like the Mayans, thought of the world in cosmological terms. Characteristic of the Aztecs' cosmology was the belief that the world moves through phases of creation and destruction. The present era, they thought, was the fifth of those cycles. They expected the world to fall apart through earthquake, and their general impression of reality was that it was inherently unstable. Aztec accounts of creation stress that it took several tries before the presiding deities got things right. Even after the world was launched, something tentative, unfinished, not fully trustworthy remained at the heart of creation.

This belief seems to have been responsible for the notorious Aztec practice of human sacrifice. We have noted that the Pawnees probably sacrificed to the Morning Star, perhaps because of Central American cultural influences. The Mayans practiced human sacrifice on occasion, but the Aztecs appear to have been the most committed to this practice. In their view, the deities running the cosmos required blood to keep it going. Blood became the currency in which human beings could trade with the gods and so assure the continuance of the Aztec regime. Potential Aztec rulers sacrificed slaves, who were usually captured in battle. As the Aztecs were a warrior people, eager to fight, slaves were readily available.

This account of Aztec human sacrifice forces the reader to confront a grisly ritual:

One of the most vivid examples of the Aztec ritual of sacrificing human beings (*tlamictiliztli*) appears in Bernal Diaz del Castillo's book *The Discovery and Conquest of Mexico* (1632). . . . Diaz del Castillo, a sergeant in Hernan Cortes's army, describes seeing his comrades, who had been captured in a recent battle, being dragged

---

[7] Leon-Portilla, 105.

by force up the steps of the temple of Coatepec by Aztec warriors and priests. As the "dismal drum" of the war god, Huitzilopochtli, mixed with the ominous sounds of shell and horn trumpets, the Aztecs decorated their captives with Aztec costumes and "with fans in their hands they forced them to dance before Huichilobos [Huitzilopochtli]." After this ceremonial preparation, we are told that the Aztecs placed the Spaniards "on their backs on some rather narrow stones which had been prepared as places for sacrifice, and with some knives they sawed open their chests and drew out their palpitating hearts and offered them to the idols that were there." Following this offering to the gods at the temple, the victims were rolled back down to the bottom of the steps where ritual experts "cut off their arms and feet and flayed the skin off the faces, and prepared it afterwards like glove leather with the beards on, and kept those for the festivals when they celebrated drunken orgies and the flesh they ate in chilimole."[8]

The apparent barbarity of human sacrifice or cannibalism may obscure the belief of traditional peoples that the gods required it, or that the tribe required replenishment of vitality and courage by way of the substance of a victim. No doubt these beliefs were carried to perverse ends. The fastidious preparation of the skin of the victims may even call to mind Nazi experiments in the death camps. Other accounts of Aztec sacrifice make it clear that a regular calendar was in place, at least at the end of the Aztec regime, that required a constant stream of blood. Most poignant are the references to ceremonies at which children were sacrificed. The gods had become so bloodthirsty that they were devouring the next generation before it had time to mature. The Aztec temples came to reek of blood, resembling slaughterhouses.

To find that this same people produced exquisite poetry and works of art filled with sadness about life's transiency only complicates our impression of Aztec religion. For example, an Aztec song laments: "I weep, I grow sad, I am only a singer; If I could only sometimes carry flowers, could adorn myself with them in the Place of the Fleshless! I am saddened. Only as a flower is man honored upon earth: an instant so brief he enjoys the flowers of spring: rejoice with them! I am saddened. I come from the house of the delicate butterflies; my song unfolds her petals: behold the myriad flowers: my heart is a motley painting."[9]

Even more confusing is this father's exhortation to his son who is about to depart for "college" (Aztec elite children attended formal schooling to learn the traditions of their culture and prepare for government service):

---

[8] David Carrasco, "Human Sacrifice: Aztec Rites," in *The Encyclopedia of Religion*, 6: 518.

[9] Laurette Séjourné, *Burning Water* (Berkeley, CA: Shambhala, 1976), 7–8.

Look thou, son, thou shalt not be honored, not obeyed and esteemed, but thou shalt be ordered, thou must be humble and despised and cast down; and if thy body gather to itself strength and pride, punish and humble it; look that thou not remember any carnal thing! . . . Look that thou not be surfeited with food, be temperate, love and practice abstinence and fasting . . . and also, my son, thou must take good care to understand our lord's books; unite thyself with the wise and clever, and those of good understanding.[10]

Other texts show Aztec penitents confessing their sins and performing austerities. Such texts counsel diligent attention to God, purity of conscience, and other traditional religious virtues. How can one square these texts with the gruesome realities of human sacrifice and other signs of great cruelty? Probably there is no way. Certainly such a corruption of human nature is no exclusive property of ancient peoples. But it does require a sober reading of traditional religious culture in Mexico.

The oral beginnings of Aztec culture carry no special import as to its bloodlust. Oral peoples seem, on the whole, no more or less violent or bloodthirsty than literate peoples. If anything, the cultural advances of the Aztec toward literacy and imperial status gave them more capacity to refine death-dealing and cruelty, somewhat as twentieth century technology has given the developed nations more capacity to wreak enormous destruction.

Incan Religion

In South America the greatest cultural development was that of the Incas, who dominated the central Andes. In the Neolithic period, hunters and agriculturalists prospered there. By about 5,000 years ago more complex cultures had evolved. For example, the Aldas built huge temples along the north coast of Peru. Various other peoples dominated the Andean region after the Aldas, culminating in the Incan empire, which held sway at the time of European conquest. In the sixteenth century C.E., the Incan empire stretched more than 4,000 miles from what is now southern Colombia to what is now south-central Chile.

The Incas did not develop a written language, but they did create an ingenious system of knot-tying to record bits of information. Moreover, the symbolism of binding and loosening knots gave them, like many other peoples, a sense of some control over an otherwise fluid, uncontrollable world:

---

[10] Sejourné, 8.

Knots are used to control a reality that is in itself abstract, fluctuating, evanescent. Guilt, time, or fate itself, by being concretized in a knot, comes under the control of the person who ties it and who thereby resolves a given situation. But it is not only determinate problems that can be resolved through the use of knots and the control they give. The complexities of an entire empire can be made manageable thanks to the use of knotted ropes. This was the case in pre-Columbian Peru, where the use of knotted ropes called *quipu* as instruments for keeping records was essential for the orderly functioning of the Inca empire. The use of the *quipu* made it possible for the *quipucamayoc* (keeper of the *quipu*) to manage the enormous mass of data collected by local officials and thereby keep tabs on the complex economic and military situation of the empire.[11]

The development of the Incan empire is a good model of how a religious rationale has often supported territorial expansion. The leader of the Incan peoples, who was called the Inca, was a semidivine figure, standing between heaven and earth as the mediator between the two realms. The greatest capital of the Incan era, the city of Cuzco, was considered the center of the cosmos:

> The expansion of Cuzco . . . was carried out in name of the superiority of its gods over those of other peoples who, once they were assimilated into the empire, left their principal idol (or its replica) in the Inca capital. The colonization, or federation, was founded on a system of reciprocity overseen by Cuzco. Certain cults and temples were richly endowed by the Inca (the title given the head of the empire); others were suppressed. The great social and religious leaders of the empire went regularly to the capital city, and the Inca brought colonies of collaborators (*mitima*) to the temple of the empire and sometimes had himself named priest of honor. The sanctuaries of the provinces paid tribute in kind to Cuzco, contributing, for example, young children to be sacrificed during the Capacocha ceremony, which was held to ensure the Inca's health and prosperity. Rites of communion were held periodically, to ensure the political and religious cohesion of the empire. Generally, these rites took place at the Temple of the Sun.[12]

The Incan kings were considered the sons of the Sun, and the empire was conceived as the Sun's domain. However, another leading Incan god, Pachacamac, shared this domain, presiding over the lowlands and the underworld. The Sun controlled the highlands and the heavens. The Temple of the Sun in Cuzco was richly adorned. Two golden pumas

[11] Giulia Piccaluga, "Knots," in *The Encyclopedia of Religion*, 8: 341.

[12] Pierre Duviols, "Inca Religion," in *The Encyclopedia of Religion*, 7: 153.

stood guard outside, and inside the walls were covered with silver and gold decorations. In the halls stood statues of early kings and queens, or occasionally mummies, as the Incas practiced mummification. A prayer to Viracocha, a personified deity who impressed the Spanish missionaries as a refined, monotheistic God, suggests the tenor of Incan piety: "O Creator, you who are at the ends of the earth, peerless, who has given being and force to men, who has said, 'Let this one be man and that one be woman.' You made them, you gave them shape, you gave them being. Let them live in health, free from danger, in peace. Wherever you may be, whether up in the heavens, below with Thunder, or with the clouds of the storm, listen to me, answer me, grant me my prayer, give us eternal life. Keep us forever in your hand. This offering, receive it, wherever you are, O Creator."[13]

It is interesting that the prayer allows Viracocha to be mysterious: the petitioner does not know where the God is. The petitioner assumes, though, that wherever he is, however he travels, the God can hear the prayers that people send forth. The many Incan gods probably represented further concretizations of this mysterious ultimate reality. People could pray more intensely, with a more vivid imagination, if they had such specific objects of focus as the sun and the moon, the storm and the wind, the vegetation springing from the earth and the constant motion of the waters. When natural disasters occurred—fires, droughts, floods, earthquakes—the Incas assumed that human errors, sins, were the cause. Thus, much of Incan ritual concentrated on appeasing the gods and trying to secure their good will.

The Incan empire was only the last native spurt of Andean cultural creativity. For nearly three millennia in that region people had farmed and built, and constructed elaborate rituals, political theories, and theologies. One of the most intriguing of the artifacts remaining from the period before white conquest is the system of "geoglyphs" (line drawings of huge scale) found near the modern town of Nazca, on the southern coast of Peru:

> Over 1,000 years ago figures, lines and geometric forms were drawn on the earth by removing the dark surface gravel to reveal the light-colored stratum below and neatly piling the gravel or stone along the edges. Anthropomorphs, animals, birds and flowers are found along with straight-line, trapezoidal and other abstract forms, as neat as if they had been made with a ruler. These markings have given rise to wildly imaginative speculation as well as to serious scholarship. The lines can be seen properly only from the air, and a number of scholars have suggested the possibility of astronomical alignment or significance, which some markings seem to have, although this has not yet been proved for the whole com-

---

[13] Duviols, 154–155.

plex. The lines may also have been sacred ritual pathways. Some lines go dead-straight for long distances; others converge on a single point. . . . [S]imilar markings . . . have been found near the Peruvian coast and in Chile. . . . The markings were probably made primarily as offerings to ancestors, or to sky or mountain gods (which shared overlapping identities). Mountain/sky gods controlled precious water in the coastal desert and had strong fertility associations.[14]

To comprehend phenomena such as these, we have to remind ourselves that nothing was more important in traditional South American life than good relations with the deities. If Andean peoples decided that the deities would like giant artworks, then giant artworks would naturally become the religious activity of choice. How the builders of the geoglyphs near Nazca managed to design for a god's-eye view is unknown. We must picture a mental world in which the divine powers were near and vivid, inspiring people to strive with all their might to construct monuments to please these deities. The Egyptian pyramids, the monuments of the Mayans and Olmecs, and many other prehistoric constructions, such as Stonehenge in England, attest to the willpower and ingenuity born of faith.

Shamanic Tribes

The anthropologist Michael Harner, during his second period of field work in 1960–61 in the Upper Amazon forest, concentrated on shamanism. In his studies of the Conibo and Jivaro tribes, it had become clear to him that key components of Amazonian tribal culture depended on shamanic visions. He decided to attempt such a vision himself.

What a white university professor experiences under the influence of hallucinogens in the Amazonian forest is not necessarily what a native would experience. On the other hand, perhaps such a professor is a better "translator" of such an experience for an American audience than a native would be. The Jivaro prepared Harner for his venture, and they seemed able to interpret his visions. He himself thought of the visions in terms of deep psychological structures being called up.

Akachu gave me the gourd cup. I tipped it up and swallowed the contents. The taste was somewhat disagreeable, yet slightly similar to green tomatoes. I felt a numbing sensation. I thought of that other drink, three years before among the Conibo, which had led me here [to the Jivaro tribe]. Was my shamanic quest worth the danger?

---

[14] Coe, Snow, and Benson, 184.

Shortly, however, even quasi-logical thought vanished as an inexpressible terror rapidly permeated my whole body. My companions were going to kill me! I must get away! I attempted to jump up, but instantly they were upon me. Three, four, an infinity of savages wrestled with me, forced me down, down, down. Their faces were above me, contorted into sly grins. Then blackness.

I was awakened by a flash of lightning followed by a thunderous explosion. The ground beneath me was shaking. I jumped up, utterly in a panic. A hurricane-like wind threw me back down on the ground. I stumbled again to my feet. A stinging rain pelted my body as the wind ripped at my clothes. Thunder and lightning exploded all around. I grasped a sapling to support myself. My companions were nowhere to be seen.

Suddenly, about two hundred feet away amidst the tree trunks, I could see a luminous form floating slowly towards me. I watched, terrified, as it grew larger and larger, resolving itself into a twisting form. The gigantic, writhing reptilian form floated directly towards me. Its body shone in brilliant hues of greens, purples, and reds, and as it twisted amid the lightning and thunder it looked at me with a strange, sardonic smile.

I turned to run, and then remembered the balsa staff [given to him for protection]. I looked down but could not see it. The serpentine creature was now only twenty feet away and towering above me, coiling and uncoiling. It separated into two overlapping creatures. They were now both facing me. The dragons had come to take me away! They coalesced back into one. I saw before me a stick about a foot long. I grabbed it, and desperately charged the monster with my stick outstretched before me. An earsplitting scream filled the air, and abruptly the forest was empty. The monster was gone. There was only silence and serenity. I lost consciousness."[15]

Out of his experiences and subsequent analyses Harner developed a theory according to which shamans are able to operate in two different worlds or fields of consciousness. They can deal with nature, their fellow human beings, and themselves in what we can call ordinary, common-sense consciousness. They can also operate in a second world or consciousness, navigating among the spectacular beasts and happenings. Even while not under the influence of drugs, the shaman can retain a sense of this second, extraordinary consciousness, which gives to the shaman a unique perception of reality.

In Harner's own terms, the distinction emerges as follows:

In engaging in shamanic practice, one moves between what I term an Ordinary State of Consciousness (OSC) and a Shamanic State of

---

[15] Michael Harner, *The Way of the Shaman* (San Francisco: Harper & Row, 1980), 15–16.

Consciousness (SSC). These states of consciousness are the keys to understanding, for example, how Carlos Castaneda [a writer on shamanism popular in the 1970s] can speak of an "ordinary reality" and a "nonordinary reality." The difference in these states of consciousness can perhaps be illustrated by referring to animals. Dragons, griffins, and other animals that would be considered "mythical" by us in OSC are "real" in the SSC. The idea that these are "mythical" animals is a useful and valid construct in OSC life, but superfluous and irrelevant in SSC experiences. "Fantasy" can be said to be a term applied by a person in the OSC to what is experienced in the SSC. Conversely, a person in the SSC may perceive the experiences of the OSC to be illusory in SSC terms. Both are right, as viewed from their own particular states of consciousness. The shaman has the advantage of being able to move between states of consciousness at will.[16]

In Mircea Eliade's monograph on shamanism,[17] which surveys the great variety of shamanic practices and symbols, the author describes shamanism as "archaic techniques of ecstasy." "Ecstasy" implies "stepping out" of ordinary consciousness. Perhaps because they relied on hallucinogens for their primary experiences, the tribes with whom Harner worked reported especially vivid ecstasies. Shamans who use dance, song, or ascetic practices such as fasting may report similar experiences, but the creatures they encounter are usually less fabulous or threatening.

For the Mehinaku of Brazil, the main function of the shaman is to heal. His training therefore prepares him for his work:

Kupatekuma, like all traditional Mehinaku shamans, did not consciously choose to become a *yetama*. His career began with an encounter with a spirit. In the course of a dream the monkey demon (Pahikuma) came to him and said, "My grandson, I will stay with you; I will be your 'pet'" . . . The following day Kupatekuma became ill and he recounted his dream to one of the village *yetama*, a shaman of great experience and reputation. He concluded that with the proper instruction Kupatekuma could become a shaman and smoker, retaining a relationship with the spirit (his "pet") that would enable him to be a curer. Two teachers now stepped forward, an established Mehinaku shaman and one of the better-known curers from the Arawaken Yawalapiti tribe. After bathing Kupatekuma in a tea made of a small hard fruit . . . they led him by the hand to the village plaza where the village shamans were awaiting him. All the women and children had already left the area and were

---

[16] Harner, xiii.

[17] See Mircea Eliade, *Shamanism* (Princeton, NJ: Princeton University Press/ Bollingen, 1971).

sequestered in their houses. Every smoker gave Kupatekuma a long thin cigar, each of which he smoked completely, often clearing his throat in the language of the spirits, calling, "He-he-he-he." Faint from the smoke, he was half-carried back to his house, where he vomited and collapsed in his hammock.

Three months of seclusion now followed. During the first day, Kupatekuma abstained from all food except a little manioc porridge. As he lay in his hammock, a gourd rattle for his future use in curing rituals was placed on his chest while his body was rubbed with a latex material from the *mangaba* tree to make his hands sensitive to the intrusive *kauki* [spirits]. After the first day, the restrictions were slightly relaxed. Each day he sat on a bench behind a seclusion barrier eating foods that made his lips sensitive to disease-causing *kauki*. Honey was the most effective, for it makes the lips and mouth supple and pliant. Painful foods, including pepper, salt, and tobacco were added to his diet to make him tough and put him in communication with the spirits. Kupatekuma tried hard to follow all the restrictions imposed upon him by his teachers, for he knew that if he ate forbidden foods, had sexual relations, walked in the sun, or permitted his family to speak loudly or unnecessarily in his presence, his medicines and tobacco would all lose their power and he would not become a skilled shaman.[18]

For other tribes, South American and North American, African and Australian, shamanism includes other functions. The flights of the shaman can become the main vehicle for revelations from the powers controlling the tribe's life. In these cases, we can say that ecstasy becomes the crux of cultural interpretation. What the shaman sees, his original vision, provides to the tribe the perspective on ordinary affairs by which it judges what is real, valuable, and significant, as well as what is of only passing importance.

Nature and Society

Through their extraordinary consciousnesses, shamans experience the world as fully alive, bursting with powerful forces. Such experience, along with the natural human desire to understand the physical world, moved Native Central and South Americans to think long and hard about nature. Typically, their thought was mythological—cast in the form of stories. Equally typically, they expanded their thought and deepened the impact it could have on their psyches by singing and dancing. Their stories demanded dramatic enactment. The tale of how the world had

---

[18] Thomas Gregor, *Mehinaku* (Chicago: University of Chicago Press, 1977), 335.

arisen provided the frame for a reenactment of the work of creation at the beginning of each new year. Other rituals, such as those for the initiation of young women and young men, drew on the creation account, which for most oral peoples was the primary myth because the way the world came into being set the pattern for all subsequent events.

Though a given myth may first appear bizarre or foreign to a person schooled in modern European thought, patient study affords an appreciation of native logic and seriousness, and sometimes even a poetic brilliance. Consider, for instance, Lawrence Sullivan's account of a typical native creation myth:

> The first stages of the creation myth of the Desana of Southern Colombia, recited on nearly all the festive occasions when groups of people gather to drink and dance, are quite mysterious. The myth is recounted dramatically by individuals or, sometimes, by groups whose members chant in unison. Dancing must wait until the recitation has ended. The first creative moment remains inscrutable—an enigma accomplished by the Sun, but not the sun that is visible. The Creator Sun is an invisible supernatural force that preexists all form, including his own. Paradoxically, in this domain of being, before the appearance of any knowable form, the invisible Sun is omniscient, omnipresent, omnipotent. The paradox continues throughout creation and into history. The uncreated Sun was a supreme state of being consisting of light that the Desana refer to as "yellow intention." Ironically, the very first instant of creation emanates from the yellow intention "without any fixed purpose guiding this act." In a sort of unplanned, or spontaneous, ejaculation, yellow intention seeped out of the supreme being unintentionally. "But once the yellow light had completed this act, the Sun set conditions for his Creation." From that moment on, the Sun Father (Page Abe) began to make a perfect world in which he planned every detail: the earth, the forests, the rivers, the animals, and the plants. "To each one he assigned the place he should live."[19]

This account of creation balances reason with something irrational or superrational. It gives a picture of how the world arose, but not a photograph—not something that would pretend to take away the mystery, which is intrinsic.

Also ingenious is the blend of the invisible and the visible, as well as of the accidental and the planned. The real Sun is not the present, visible sun. In the beginning the ultimate reality or source was so different from what human beings can know or find familiar that the Sun involved was radically Other. All power reposed in him, all knowledge and presence. Why yellow intention should have seeped from him is unclear—to the Desana as well as ourselves. Presumably the symbolism relates the origin

---

[19] Lawrence E. Sullivan, *Icanchu's Drum* (New York: Macmillan, 1988), 29–30.

of the present natural world to human procreation, which requires the flow of bodily fluids. Having issued his creative power, however, the Sun Father went on to care for his creation. Because he assigned all creatures their proper places, the Desana can be confident that the world is in good order.

The human need to know that the world is not chaotic is a major motive for accounts of creation. Even as they confess that they cannot understand the ultimate reasons for creation, humans need to feel that enough order is available to protect them from chaos. The natural world stimulated oral peoples, as it stimulates present-day scientific peoples, to find patterns and hypotheses to bring it under control. Once people secure from nature the means of survival, they inevitably fall to thinking about how nature works in its own right. The Desana were typical not only in speculating about the origin of the world but in reciting regularly their conception of it.

The constant pattern across all native societies of Central and South America was the effort to link the origins and present being of the people with the origins and present being of the cosmos. Whether the people venerated a king or a quasi-divine being or relied on shamans for periodic contact with the ultimate powers, their religious thought was fully political. How their societies were organized, how they deployed power, what their social ranks signified—all were functions of their basic beliefs about the structures built into the cosmos by the Creator. Again and again, we find that even the smallest group thinks of itself as the center of creation. The world emanates, is organized outward, from the tribe's town, or from the imperial capital. The aim of astronomical calculations is to chart the history of the particular society. The function of priests is to create, maintain, keep plausible the myths and rituals that support the theology and thus the political structure. For a people to maintain the coherence of its culture, political and cosmological thought must be in sync.

The Self and Divinity

The individual member of a shamanic culture was bound to think of selfhood in ecstatic terms. What came into the shaman's ecstatic view had the greatest say about crucial matters like sickness and death, the meaning of life, and the ways of the sacred powers. Many tribes were also greatly concerned with social relations, charting carefully the blood ties of families, in large part to control intermarriage. Individuals were also brought up to know their physical environment intimately. Recognizing varieties of plants and trees, learning the ways of game animals, knowing the usual patterns of rivers (when they flooded and how much) was all necessary if people were to thrive in their given habitat.

The selfhood of a person growing up in a traditional, shamanic tribe also depended greatly on myths and rituals. The individual had to take to heart the tribe's ways, its customs and beliefs, to survive. The way to distinction in the tribe was to become an outstanding hunter or fighter, a great weaver or potter. Tribal leaders were revered for their strength, but even more for their practical wisdom. Elders might not be chiefs, but their store of mythological and ritual knowledge could give them high status. Women tended to rank below men in status, yet the ability of women to give birth remained an awesome power. Without women the tribe had no future.

In the more developed cultures of Central and South America, the self was subject to more extensive controls. Because the empires supported standing armies, in large part to extend their territories rather than to dominate their own people, the rulers usually had the means to enforce their laws. The blend of religious and political power vested in the kings and high priests led to a significant distinction between commoners and nobles. The bulk of the people were peasant farmers or artisans. The elite few controlled priestly rituals, sacred lore, and imperial administrative power.

In both smaller and larger traditional societies, a certain stylization of sexual roles tended to be the rule. Sexual interactions had to fit into a cosmic scheme according to which procreation was a very objective part of nature's economy. Relations between men and women therefore probably were less "personal" than those of modern Western culture. Individual fulfillment was not as pressing a concern; people married to continue the tribe.

Traditional societies were true to their name in their reverence of the past as a golden age. The past was closer to the time of creation, when the basic patterns of life were established. Over time culture, if not the entire cosmic order, had tended to wobble out of place. Maintaining the traditional myths and ceremonies was therefore crucial.

The gods, too, continued to be what they had been since the time of creation, for they had kept the world and the tribe going. Enough ambiguity was built into the characteristics of the gods to ensure explanations of new natural or social phenomena, but the stability of the gods was all-important. One could depend on the stories about them to explain how the world worked, why people lived and died, how human beings and animals ought to interact.

The considerable variety of religious life found among peoples of South America depends greatly on the physical area in which they live. Their ceremonies have been efforts to placate the forces they thought controlled the jungle or the mountains, the crops or the animals. Common to all is the instinct to believe that the world is more than what meets the eye, and that the spiritual side of any phenomenon is more important than its physical side. Thus, whether through shamanic practices or priestly rituals, the natives of South America and Central America have professed themselves to be people intimately bound to the gods, the spiritual powers, of their native places. They have loved and feared their traditional forest or mountain region because it was alive with powers of life and death, good and evil. Contending with such powers has been the basic business of their cultures.

Study Questions

1. Why would a contemporary Mexican peasant like Juan expect revelations through his dreams?
2. What was the significance of the Olmec were-jaguar?
3. Why were the Mayans so interested in astronomy and developing an extensive calendar?
4. Explain the function of human sacrifice in Aztec culture.
5. In what sense was the Temple of the Sun the center of Incan culture?
6. How does the South American shaman's second, nonordinary consciousness affect his ordinary consciousness?
7. Why is a creation myth so important to so wide a variety of cultures?

CHAPTER 4

Native Africans

Overview

The history of African peoples living south of the Sahara is obscure, in part because Christianity and Islam have reshaped native traditions. Prior to the coming of Christianity and Islam, local religions thrived. Indeed, since there are more than 700 languages in this area, one may speak of a profusion of local traditions. Religious practices tended to be similar within linguistic families, and across the entire Sub-Sahara region a few general attitudes have prevailed among Native Africans.

What is known about the history of human beings in Africa depends on sketchy artifactual remains. The climate did not favor the preservation of most cultural products. Paleontologists working from skeletal remains favor Africa as the site where the predecessors of our species, *Homo sapiens*, developed millions of years ago, but the history of that development, including the history of true human beings during the Stone Age, is vague at best.

Rock paintings found in southern Africa suggest a continuous activity of shamans for the past 25,000 years or so. Some of these paintings date from the nineteenth century, but the oldest go back tens of millennia. Current interpretation of the paintings makes them out to be depictions of what shamans have experienced in trance. The shamanic figures are related to the major game animal of the area, a large antelope. The paintings show shamans bleeding from the nose, sweating, dancing, wearing caps of animal skin, and being transformed into half-antelopes. The paintings' depictions largely fit the patterns of shamanic activity that we have seen in the Americas.

Interpreters assume that the rock paintings reflect the activities through which shamans went into trance, as well as what they experienced while in trance. The major activities of shamans in this area, documented from recent times, have been securing game, healing sickness, and bringing rain. Various paintings portray shamans involved in all these activities. For example, they are shown bending over sick people and drawing out the cause of the illness. They are also shown shooting special animals that are presumed to be the source of rain. Clearly, hunters of this area identified closely with the animals on whom their fate depended. They also needed sufficient rain for the plants they gathered to grow. African thought has held that in trance shamans experience a sacred power. The antelope also possess this power, so trance facilitates the bonding with antelopes on which shamans depend. The current scholarly opinion is that shamanic trance, to which the main pathway is dancing, has been the religious center of tribal life in southern Africa.

With the spread of agriculture south of the Sahara about 3,500 years ago, local, territorial religious cults developed. People became more interested in the flora of their given area and less inclined to wander in pursuit of game. At local shrines priests specialized in the fertility rites thought necessary to ensure good crops in the given locale. They sought ways of bringing rain and could become healers as a further extension of their power to secure well-being and fertility.

About 1,500 years ago Africans learned the art of working iron, and that development also brought religious changes. Myths, rituals, and purification practices came to surround iron-working to explain where the magical metal had come from, how best to handle it, and how smiths ought to comport themselves. The singularly hard metal was both an immortal element—a victor over ordinary death and decay—and a fearsome source of death when worked into weapons. The smith had clear connections to the hunter and the warrior, who both inflicted death. African myth and ritual reflect a deep concern with the relations of people, materials, and death.

Ancient sculptures in both terra cotta and bronze depicting animals and human beings have been found in Nigeria. The heads of what are conjectured to be Nigerian kings, found near the royal palace at Ife, remind us that the king was a sacral figure in traditional African cultures as in virtually all others, including medieval European. Nigerian religious thought located the power of a person in the head, which carried the person's destiny. The destiny of a king, for example, was to wear a crown. The crown became the key symbol or metaphor for kingship. Kings mediated between heaven and earth. The vitality of the people, including that of their crops, depended on the vitality of the king. When the king began to lose his vigor, he could be slain to make way for a younger, more virile leader. Because fertility and good health were key signs of divine favor, most religious rituals pursued them.

Some scholars of African religion note that native rituals have not been otherworldly; by and large, African religious activity has not sought personal immortality. The various rites are based on the assumption that human wrongdoing is responsible for ill fortune, including sickness, and therefore attempt to overcome wrongdoing and restore balance. The individual is a combination of spiritual, physical, social, and natural relations. The sickness of the individual threatens the tribe; in turn, the wrongdoing of the tribe can make an individual fall ill, make women infertile, or cause drought.

The main religious functionaries to share sacred status with kings, though not royal power, are prophets, who tell the future or call people to account for their moral failures; priests, who make sacrifices (usually of grains or animals) to get the gods' attention; and diviners, who determine why a given state of affairs (usually unfortunate) has come about. These functionaries have mediated between the people and the gods, but any political influence they have exerted has been attributable to their personal qualities rather than to their offices.

Most traditional African tribes have sponsored rites of passage—ceremonies to pace the person through the life cycle. The key moments in the life cycle are birth, coming of age, marriage, adulthood, death, and ancestorhood. Dreams have been a powerful source of revelation through which ancestors could speak. Traditional Africans tried to maintain close relations with the departed. They feared that the dead who were not at rest would haunt them as ghosts.

Traditional African religious thought has combined elements of mono- and polytheism. Many peoples pictured a singular ultimate deity responsible for the creation of the world and available if either the world or an individual should come into crisis. This high god otherwise had little to do with daily affairs, which were the province of numerous, more specialized, local divinities. One prayed to these local divinities and sacrificed to them for pragmatic benefits such as a cure, a view of the future, good crops, a good hunt, or children. The high god stayed in the background. The local gods were the focus of ordinary religious rituals.[1]

Mountain People and Forest People

The Ik, a tribe of hunters and cattle-tenders who traditionally roamed areas now located in Kenya and Uganda, have become infamous in anthropological lore because of studies carried out by Colin Turnbull, a British anthropologist, in the 1960s. He described a people so uprooted from their traditional way of life that their society had broken down. Individuals had become completely selfish, looking out for themselves only, because bare essentials such as food and shelter had become scarce.

[1] See Benjamin C. Ray, "African Religions: An Overview," in *The Encyclopedia of Religion*, ed. Mircea Eliade (New York: Macmillan, 1987), 1:60–69.

The only remnant of an older, more decent Ician society lay in the attitude of a few aged people toward Mount Morungole, the traditional home of the creator god Didigwari. According to legend, long ago Didigwari lowered the first human beings from heaven on a vine at Lomej, at the foot of Mount Morungole. They were large and strong. He gave them the digging stick (perhaps the most important African tool) and forbade them to kill one another. When the men refused to share the game they had killed with the women, Didigwari became angry and withdrew his vine. Ever since, God has been far from human beings, and the Ik have never felt they could hunt at the foot of the mountain.

> While Mount Morungole itself has no such legends attached to it by the Ik, it none the less figures in their ideology and is in some ways regarded by them as sacred. I had noticed this by the almost reverential way in which they looked at it—none of the shrewd cunning and cold appraisal with which they regarded the rest of the world, animate and inanimate. When they talked about it too there was a different quality to their voices, and I found this still to be so long after I had given up expecting anything among the Ik comparable to our notions of what is good and beautiful and truthful. They seemed incapable of talking about Morungole in any other way, which is probably why they talked about it so very seldom.[2]

For a moment Turnbull glimpsed how things might have been, as little as a generation earlier, when the Ik had roamed freely over what they considered their ancestral land. Political disputes and ambitions in Uganda and Kenya had dislocated them, causing their entire culture to fall into crisis. Without access to a supply of food, life had become impossibly competitive. Parents no longer cared for their children. Being unable to provide for them, the parents often had to see them die as infants, and therefore had closed down their emotional attachments. They no longer let themselves feel love, pity, or interest for the elderly. Where most African peoples revered the elderly as precious sources of wisdom, the Ik begrudged spending resources on either elders or children. In this context, the reverence accorded to Mount Morungole suggests how deeply rooted is the need for something sacred. Turnbull's study of the Ik is a chilling reminder that physical well-being has direct effects on spiritual well-being. People who are starving can lose elementary decencies.

The BaMbuti, a Pygmy people of the Congo forest, live a good distance from the mountains of the Ik. What stands out when one compares the two peoples, though, is their dependence on their environments. Just as the Ik had through the centuries become mountain people, their lives shaped by the game available in their region, so the BaMbuti had

---

[2] Colin M. Turnbull, *The Mountain People* (New York: Simon and Schuster, 1972), 187–188.

become forest people, shaped by the resources of their jungle habitat. Indeed, the BaMbuti had lived so long in the tropical forest that their visual perception had become adapted to it: Never seeing things at a far distance or experiencing an open vista, they did not know how to calculate size. One of Turnbull's informants, Kenge, on his first trip out of the forest, was amazed to be able to see for miles, unimpeded by the forest. He thought animals grazing in the distance were tiny, on the order of insects.

The Pygmies were a much happier people than the Ik. When Turnbull studied them in the early 1960s, he came away much impressed by the cooperative way of life they had evolved. They had their troubles and quarrels, but essentially they felt that the forest had been good to them. Indeed, one of the touching aspects of their culture was the song they would sing on many nights to the forest, using a long, tubular instrument called a *molimo*.

To sing the molimo was equivalent to celebrating the forest, even worshiping it. It was a ritual of thanksgiving, praise, blessing. As Turnbull puts it, "It was as though the nightly chorus were an intimate communion between a people and their god, the forest." One of the Pygmies told Turnbull "how all Pygmies have different names for their god, but how they all know that it is really the same one. Just what it is, of course, they don't know, and that is why the name really does not matter very much. 'How can we know?' he asked. 'We can't see him; perhaps only when we die will we know and then we can't tell anyone. . . . But he must be good to give us so many things. He must be of the forest. So when we sing, we sing to the forest.'"[3]

African Rituals

The BaMbuti faith in the forest became especially poignant at times of death. Then the Pygmies would outdo themselves in singing special praises to the forest. Even at death they remained optimistic: If the forest knew of their pain, it would be sure to hasten to help them. From time to time the forest fell asleep, as all living things must. The molimo would awaken the forest, bring it back to awareness with delightful song. Then the forest would again give the BaMbuti good, right, sound, and beautiful things.

The Pygmies' positive attitude toward the forest, and toward the whole of life, extended to their attitude toward girls' coming of age. For village Africans, living outside the forest, bloodshed of any kind was an abomination, something to be feared. The Pygmies, by contrast, cele-

---

[3] Colin M. Turnbull, *The Forest People* (New York: Simon and Schuster, 1962) 92–93.

brated a happy ritual called the *elima*, marking when girls first began to be "blessed by the moon."

The seclusion into which village girls were forced at puberty was full of negative emotions and fears. On the contrary,

> in the house of the elima the girls celebrate the happy event together. Together they are taught the arts and crafts of motherhood by an old and respected relative. They learn not only how to live like adults, but how to sing the songs of adult women. Day after day, night after night, the elima house resounds with the throaty contralto of the older women and the high, piping voices of the youngest. It is a time of gladness and happiness, not for the women alone but for the whole people. Pygmies from all around come to pay their respects, the young men standing or sitting about outside the elima house in the hopes of a glimpse of the young beauties inside. And there are special elima songs which they sing to one another, the girls singing a light, cascading melody in intricate harmony, the men replying with a rich, vital chorus. For the Pygmies the elima is one of the happiest, most joyful occasions in their lives.[4]

The place of song in Pygmy culture reminds us of the key role of the shaman's song in other oral cultures, where the song epitomized the shaman's deepest self. Here we witness the social dimension of song. It is natural for the young women and men to package themselves in song and use it to give and receive. Coming of age represents the basic mystery that the BaMbuti find all-absorbing: the power of life come into the young girls' bodies for a time overshadows the hunt or any other activity. A positive view of sexuality emerges from this celebration. It is no wonder that the fertility of women and men, along with their mutual attraction and cooperation, has stood at the center of traditional Pygmy life.

Africans are known for their ritualization of the life cycle. Their sense that time ought to be a progressive initiation into the mysteries of life and death is not unique among oral peoples, but it does stand out as especially impressive. Tribes such as the Ndembu of Zambia have also evolved rituals to deal with sickness and bewitchment. For example, Victor Turner, a cultural anthropologist, has written of the Ndembu rituals *Ihamba* and *Kaneng'a*:

> *Ihamba* is the name not only of the ritual but also of the afflicting agency, in this case the shade [ghost] of a dead hunter, which is thought to inhere in one of the two upper front incisors of the dead man. . . . Under the influence of the shade, the tooth is believed to fly about invisibly and to fix itself in the body of a living relative of the dead hunter. In this way it punishes a person who has failed to pour out a libation of blood or beer to the shade of the deceased,

---

[4] Turnbull, *The Forest People*, 187.

who has "forgotten the shade in his heart," or who has offended the shade by quarrelling with his kinsfolk. . . . Much depends on the moral condition of the patient and of his group in determining whether the hunter's shade will allow the tooth to be removed. . . . *Kaneng'a* is performed to cure persons bewitched by the living. A male sorcerer or a female witch causes severe illness by sending familiars [spirits in his or her power] against his or her kin. The *Kaneng'a* specialist aims either to drive away these familiars from the patients, or to force their owners to call them off by the threat of public exposure.[5]

These Ndembu rituals adhere to the patterns of shamanic healing and exorcism that we have seen in the Americas. The tooth that can travel, enter the body of a person who has not properly revered a ghost, and provoke illness recalls the afflicting element that Native American shamans tried to suck out or draw up from sick people. The belief that unless the dead are treated well and honored appropriately they will return to cause mischief is widespread in both North and Latin America.

In traditional cultures of the Americas as well as Africa ancestors are living entities much more than distant memories. The world has a distinct place for the departed. They do not simply go into the ground and disappear. They continue to function in the overall system of the cosmos, partaking in the comprehensive patterns of living and dying. Moreover, they witness to the significance of spiritual powers, as do the malign influences of witches. The ability to send familiars (which in the Americas would be tied to animals honored by a given tribe) against one's foes stems from witches' or sorcerers' intercourse with the spiritual world. The curer who would protect people against bewitchment must have equally strong standing in the spiritual world, though the assumption is that he or she works with good spirits to offset the plans of evil human beings and their familiars.

Oral peoples appreciate the role of intention: It is not just what we do, but also what we want to do, that determines who we really are. Africans and other traditional oral peoples have tried to address evil intentions by reassuring the individual afflicted by them that good intentions can offset them. Behind traditional African rituals of curing lies the belief that to hate evil is to desire good, to fight sickness is to defend health. The intimate, delicate relations between the body and the spirit—the one can sicken if the other is afflicted—mirrors the larger relationships between people, and between the individual and the group. If one person is disordered, the whole group suffers. If the whole group is chasing unworthy goals, individuals are bound to feel ill effects. African wisdom stems from this foundation of holistic thinking.

---

[5] Victor Turner, *The Drums of Affliction* (Ithaca, NY: Cornell University Press, 1981), 114–115.

African Myths

As we might expect, the rich retinue of African rituals is matched by that of African myths. African theology, philosophy, psychology, political science, and medicine have all been embedded in stories. From time out of mind ancestors have handed down traditional wisdom about how the world arose, the nature of the human being, where sickness comes from and how healers can make it depart. Many of these stories are remarkably imaginative. Told and retold for generations, brooded upon by tribal elders, they can swell to fantastic proportions, creating a thought-world of great complexity.

The anthropologist Marcel Griaule discovered the complexity of the Dogon thought-world when he was accepted as an initiate by the blind Dogon elder Ogotemmeli. Ogotemmeli was revered in his neighborhood as a wise man. For years Ogotemmeli had contemplated the stories in which the Dogon had cast their conception of the universe. At the end of more than a month of instruction, Griaule realized that he was just scratching the surface of this traditional worldview. Many of the notions that Ogotemmeli laid out for him were so strange that it took him a long time to discover their logic. To the average Westerner, especially one trained academically in scientific methods, the order of the Dogon universe seemed haphazard. The Dogon associated things as much because of accidental similarity in shape, color, or other qualities as because of intrinsic causal relations.

Griaule describes Ogotemmeli at work on the second day of Griaule's initiation, after they have made contact and established the course of instruction they will pursue:

> It was essential to begin with the dawn of all things. [Ogotemmeli] rejected as a detail of no interest, the popular account of how the fourteen solar systems were formed from flat circular slabs of earth one on top of the other. He was only prepared to speak of the serviceable solar system; he agreed to consider the stars, though they only played a secondary part.
>
> "It is quite true," he said, "that in course of time women took down the stars to give them to their children. The children put spindles through them and made then spin like fiery tops to show themselves how the world turned. But that was only a game."
>
> The stars came from pellets of earth flung out into space by the God Amma, the one God. He had created the sun and the moon by a more complicated process, which was not the first known to man but is the first attested invention of God: the art of pottery. The sun is, in a sense, a pot raised once for all to white heat and surrounded by a spiral of red copper with eight turns. The moon is the same shape, but its copper is white. It was heated only one quarter at a time. Ogotemmeli said he would explain later the movements of

these bodies. For the moment he was concerned only to indicate the main lines of the design, and from that to pass to its actors.

He was anxious, however, to give an idea of the size of the sun. "Some," he said, "think it is as large as this encampment, which would mean thirty cubits. But it is really bigger. Its surface area is bigger than the whole of Sanga Canton." And after some hesitation he added: "It is perhaps even bigger than that." He refused to linger over the dimensions of the moon, nor did he ever say anything about them. The moon's function was not important, and he would speak of it later. He said however that, while Africans were creatures of light emanating from the fullness of the sun, Europeans were creatures of the moonlight: hence their immature appearance."[6]

Ogotemmeli takes it for granted that the notions he is exposing are lucid, sensible, vouched for by tradition. He is aware of variations in traditional Dogon interpretation, but sufficient for the moment is a relatively straightforward description of how the world came into being. As is typical of oral peoples, he locates the present order of the world in the cosmogonic myth—the story of how the world arose. He is most interested in the sun, because the sun is the ancestor of the African people, less so in the stars and the moon. Because copper is the key metal in the area of the Dogon, it is natural for copper to be the material from which both the sun and the moon were formed. The notion that Europeans are creatures of the moonlight reminds us that there are two sides to every cross-cultural encounter: if early European explorers found Africans very strange, the reverse was equally true.

In West Africa many tribes, including the Dogon, structure their traditional mythology in terms of 266 signs. These signs are the seeds of all knowledge. Somewhat like Chinese ideograms, African signs make for "idea-writing." The signs generate all creatures, too, and so are part of the traditional cosmogony. They themselves issue from a single sign, which symbolizes the unity and multiplicity of the Creator. The French writer Germaine Dieterlin explains it this way:

> This idea . . . conditions all representations tied to the creation of the universe. The universe came out of a word, the spirit and thought of a creator God who first brought forth, out of nothing, "signs" that designated in advance all that was to make up creation. Then God created matter in the form of an initial placenta on the walls of which were engraved the first signs of beings and things (eight seeds and two pairs of mixed twins, the prototypes of future man). It follows that what are ordinarily called "spiritual principles" were at first conceived only as the essence of signs inscribed in the initial placenta, or "womb" of God. That is why the 266 basic signs

---

[6] Marcel Griaule, *Conversations with Ogotemmeli* (New York: Oxford University Press, 1972), 16–17.

correspond to the number of days totaling the nine months required for human gestation. Here as elsewhere in black Africa, the connection between the biological plane and the cosmogonic system is self-evident.[7]

The scheme described by Dieterlin focuses on primary or constituent signs and on gestation. The world grows in the womb of God—a correspondence to the Great Mother venerated in many parts of the world. But prior even to the womb was the word, and prior to that—nothing. The idea of nothingness has played a variety of roles in the religious systems of peoples the world over and throughout time, attesting to the human fascination with origins.

East African Traditions

Let us turn from a West African picture of creation to East African ideas about evil. The usual East African understanding of evil relates it to witchcraft. The Azande of the southwestern Sudan, for example, speak of both witchcraft and sorcery. Witches can cause harm to people simply by thinking about or willing it. Sorcerers use material agents to work mischief.

The community is all-important in traditional East African groups, wherein people form intense emotional bonds. The witch is a deviant, defective member of the community, and witchcraft ruptures those bonds, subverts them with bad intentions. If something has gone wrong—sickness, sadness, loss of wealth—the East African instinct is that someone has willed this misfortune. Events do not simply happen, they are chosen, carried out by an intentional agent. An enemy (in the case of bad events) or a friend (in the case of good events) has willed them into being.

The source of misfortune, it is usually assumed, comes from within the circle of familiar, known people.

> Their motivation is held to be hatred, envy, and jealousy against those who are more fortunate or successful. These emotions are felt toward others who are already known; it is extremely rare that such feelings are provoked by strangers. Their identity depends largely on the composition of the more important groups whose members should regard themselves as a community. Witchcraft is a kind of treachery, a perversion for ignoble ends of proper authority, obligation, and affection. Thus where the basic local group is a kinship

---

[7] Germaine Dieterlin, "Graphic Signs and the Seed of Knowledge," in *Mythologies*, Comp. Yves Bonnefoy (Chicago: University of Chicago Press, 1991), 1:30.

one, witches are held to be kin of their victims and sorcerers are thought to harm unrelated persons. Where such kin groups are unimportant, the distinction between witches and sorcerers may not be made.

These beliefs are linked to knowledge of technical causation. . . . It is clear that a man is gored by a buffalo; the belief in witchcraft is used to explain not that he was gored as such but why he was gored by a particular animal at that particular time and place. The identity of the witch is discovered by divination, and demands for reparation, vengeance, punishment, or other socially approved action can be taken by the community so as to restore proper relations between the concerned parties. The whole is an effective jural process once the premises are accepted.[8]

The Zande people's belief in witchcraft allows them to work out their hostilities. If some people are resentful of others' prosperity, attributing misfortune to the witchcraft of the prosperous people can become a way of dealing with group tensions. If the prosperous people have gotten their gains unfairly, the instinct of the community may well be to accept the charge of witchcraft against the prosperous and see to their punishment—that is, to restore a condition of fairness. If, however, the accused are not really guilty of any wrongdoing, the case becomes more complicated, and the chance arises that innocent people will be wronged.

In addition to its sociological function, witchcraft provides a way to explain many evils. Rather than confront the frightening fact that misfortune can just happen, without rhyme or reason, East Africans and many other traditional peoples have concentrated on what can be known: human feelings, desires to cause good or evil. Blaming and praising intentions, however strange a practice it may appear to outsiders, lends a sense of coherence to the community. The goring of a man by a buffalo is not a meaningless accident; it is better to confront a known enemy than an unknowable, diabolical mystery.

The Bantu-speaking peoples of East Africa are typical of many oral peoples on many continents in having a divine Creator who is distant from the world. (An exception are the Kikuyu, whose creator shapes daily affairs, personal and communal alike, and so is the focus of ritual activities.) For the Nyoro, Ruhanga, the Creator, made the world and gave human beings everything they needed to survive. The structure of Nyoro society came from Ruhanga, so the current division into farmers, cattle-herders, and rulers has a divine stamp of approval. Ruhanga had three sons, the prototypes of the members of these three social classes. He tested them, and because they passed his test each of the classes, each of the kinds of work, is trustworthy. The problems in Nyoro culture stem

---

[8] John Middleton, "East African Religions: An Overview," in *The Encyclopedia of Religion*, 4:547.

from Ruhanga's fourth son, Kantu, who turned bad, introduced evil into the world, and corrupted the human heart. Ruhanga was so disappointed that he withdrew to a remote part of heaven, sending death and disease as punishments. Nyoro ritual aims at containing these punishments. It does not deal with Ruhanga, however, because he continues to be remote, displeased with humankind.[9] It must focus on lesser gods.

This story amounts to an African version of original sin. The Nyoro way of life—farming, cattle-herding, serving as kings—would have pleased the Creator. But the Nyoro people have been corrupted. Parallel to the Christian doctrine of original sin, the Nyoro mythology leaves human beings an out: none of the historical generations chose to become alienated from God. Each has been the victim of a preexisting state of affairs. Thus human beings may be excused for leaving the estimation of their worth in the hands of the judge who knows what happened in the beginning.

South African Themes

It is not known precisely how traditional Africans lived prior to the coming of whites. This is true of South Africa, where whites have been a transforming presence for centuries. Raymond Cowles, a naturalist, has extrapolated from what is known about the ecological history of the area to reconstruct traditional South African life as follows:

> For uncounted centuries the tall grasses of the South African valleys—the Umzumbe, the Umzumkulu, the Umkomasi, the Umvoti, and others—had reached shoulder height, and at the end of the rainy season the long-horned native cattle were almost buried in growing fodder. Still later, Zulu invaders, as sleek as their cattle, leisurely tended their herds, and their small but adequate gardens of milo maize, "taro," squash, beans, and ground nuts, but most important, maize. From the product of their grain crops the warm, leisurely months of winter were filled with feasting and the revelry of beer drinks.
>
> Except for the occasional but recurrent murderous raids and petty wars initiated by their Zulu brethren to the northeast, life was outwardly peaceful and contented, rich in material things needed to gladden the hearts of these people. Nonetheless, fear remained an invisible canker in this Eden: There were senseless fears based on superstitions, and real fears of the death that could be meted out to anyone who might be accused of witchcraft. There was the

[9] Benjamin C. Ray, "East African Religions: Northeastern Bantu Religions," In *The Encyclopedia of Religion*, 4:552.

ever-present fear for the death of loved ones at the hands of sorcerers. There was also the fear of old age and infirmity when one had lost his usefulness and would be turned out into the bush to die. Death as infanticide, parricide, murder, accident of the hunt or in the fields, and incessant wars and raids kept the population small over the centuries. Beyond these dangers pervading the valleys even then, was the fear that in prolonged droughts, famine and disease might decimate the families. Nonetheless the inhabitants of the valleys had less to fear than others on less fertile soil.[10]

The author suggests that women were worse off than men because women had to do more of the manual labor and the societal structure was polygamous—a man could have several wives. Even for women, however, material conditions were good, pleasures were many, and fears tended to focus on the unknown: disease, accident, drought, attack. When whites came to South Africa, they conquered lands held by the Zulu, imposing their own economic and cultural controls. Missionaries, educators, and doctors sought to change the traditional Zulu way of life. At first they had little success, but gradually the impact of white culture made for new living conditions. Most significant, in Cowles's view, were the shifts in what had been a balanced ecology. White medicines reduced infant deaths and prolonged the lives of many adults. As the population grew, the land became overplanted, overfarmed. The worn land eroded more easily, was more damaged by both drought and flood. The herds began to suffer. Soon the land would not support the people using it.

When investigating traditional African cultures, we can never be sure that we have accounted for all the changes that white influence, proximate or remote, has introduced. The ecology of a given people's habitat was crucial during the millennia when they lived in close contact with the land. The superstructure of Western culture—institutions of learning, business, medicine, government, communications, and so on—that now shape our sense of the world had no parallel among traditional, oral peoples. We can be certain, however, that the vast majority of the people concerned themselves with primary matters of survival: obtaining food and shelter, begetting and raising children, warding off enemies such as death, illness, and rapacious neighbors. Natural forces tended to create a balance between a human population and its habitat. If too many people tried to live in a given valley, many died or saw that they had to move.

This sketch of traditional Zulu life captures much of its essential simplicity. In a fertile habitat, the people could create a relatively easy, enjoyable life, though they had to deal with their fears of the unknown, of disease and death, and of destructive human impulses. In evaluating traditional cultures, it is important to examine their individual concepts

---

[10] Raymond B. Cowles, *Zulu Journal* (Berkeley: University of California Press, 1959), 260–261.

of ease and hardship, joy and fear. It is equally important to study how myth and ritual affected the way they balanced pleasure and pain, joy and sorrow. If such people found reasons to be glad they had been born, to praise the powers that had brought them and their world into being, we ought to respect, perhaps envy them in some ways, because an honest look at our own cultures shows that such a positive evaluation of the human condition is no easy accomplishment.

We are on surer ground when we study the stories and ceremonies of traditional South Africans, which reveal a sense of humor that may be the key to the best parts of native cultures. For example, a story explaining how the hippo got his stumpy tail shows the interest that native South Africans have taken in the animals of their habitat and the wit with which they have observed them:

Once the rabbit came to the elephant and proposed a test of strength. The elephant, lord of the local animals, laughed at the little rabbit. But the rabbit persevered, demanding to be taken seriously. They would have a tug-of-war, he proposed. The elephant would stand on the bank of the river, the rabbit would go down to the water. Each would hold onto an end of a rope. When the rabbit gave two tugs, the elephant would commence hauling. He would be surprised to learn how strong rabbits can be.

The elephant had little to do, so he indulged the rabbit. The rabbit left the rope and hustled down the bank to the water. There he spoke with the hippo, proposing another test of strength. The hippo was as unimpressed by the little rabbit as the elephant had been, but he too finally agreed. The rabbit told him to take up an end of the rope and wait for the signal: two tugs.

Returning half-way up the bank, and seeing that the rope, hung between the elephant and the hippo (who could not see one another), was taut, the rabbit gave two tugs and sat back to enjoy the battle of the giants. The elephant was amazed. How could the rabbit, so small, resist him? The hippo was astonished: here was strength more than a match for his own. They set to work in earnest, but of course the hippo was no match for the mighty elephant. Soon the hippo was over the hump of the bank, being hauled up by the elephant.

When he saw who his actual adversary was, the elephant was peeved. The rabbit had tricked him, he knew, but the hippo must have been in cahoots. For his part, the hippo was trembling. It was a terrible thing to encounter the wrath of the lord elephant. He tried to explain that he thought he was pulling against the rabbit, but the elephant took that as an insult. How could the hippo expect him to believe such an absurdity. Blazing with anger, he gave the hippo two choices: die, or have his tail cut off. The hippo tried to run, but the elephant quickly caught him and, seizing a knife nearby, cut off his tail. When the hippo got home, he felt disgraced. So he called his whole household and decreed that they all cut off their tails. Since that time, hippos have had stumpy tails.[11]

Like folk stories about the tortoise and the hare, or the mouse and the lion, this story gave people the chance to think about the great variety of creatures in their locale, to account for their various attributes—whether strength, quick-wittedness, or stolidity. In places where life was relatively easy, stories enhanced delight and the sense of good fortune. And, subtly, they introduced a sense of superiority, of pride in being human. Human beings were the only species that could step back and tell stories about the other animals. Indeed, they could step back from their fellow human beings, from the gods, and from themselves, and take delight in what they saw.

Nature and Society

The Zulus provide another instance of traditional oral peoples' relation to nature, an intimate connection to the cycles of the physical cosmos. They did not separate themselves from the natural world as so many modern Westerners have. They were not anthropocentric. Their lives depended on the maize and cattle. Good relations with the animals and plants of their locale, the winds and rains, were essential to their survival. As droughts increased in South Africa, the people became uneasy. What was responsible for this turning of the gods against them? What enemy or malign force was seeking their ruin?

We modern peoples may sometimes be equally helpless before natural disasters—droughts and floods, hurricanes and tornadoes—but we do not think of ourselves as immersed in the natural world. We do not feel that natural disasters are the turning against us of fellow forces. So we must struggle to imagine the sensitivity with which groups like the Zulu watched and listened. We must work to understand why witchcraft and sorcery were a natural expression of deep fears that someone was interfering with the proper operation of the natural world.

For certain African peoples a special connection with a particular animal or place colors the entire culture. The Nuer of the southern Sudan, for example, have this tie to cattle. E. E. Evans-Pritchard, in a study of Nuer religion, describes the general relations between Nuer and their cattle:

> Nuer are very largely dependent on the milk of their herds, and in their harsh environment they probably could not live without them,

---

[11] A. C. Jordan, *Tales from Southern Africa* (Berkeley: University of California Press, 1978), 263–265.

any more than the cattle could live without the care and protection of their owners. Their carcasses also furnish Nuer with meat, tools, ornaments, sleeping-hides, and various other objects of domestic use; and their sun-dried dung provides fuel for the great smoldering smudges that give protection from mosquitoes to man and beast alike. Women are more interested in the cows, and this is natural for they have charge of milking and dairy work. Men's interest in the cows is, apart from their values for breeding, rather for their use in obtaining wives, and they are interested in the oxen for the same reason, and also because they provide them with a means of display and . . . sacrifice. But for all Nuer—men, women, and children—cattle are their great treasure, a constant source of pride and joy, the occasion also of much foresight, anxiety, and quarrelling; and they are their intimate companions from birth to death. It is not difficult to understand, therefore, that Nuer give their cattle devoted attention, and it is not surprising that they talk more of cattle than of anything else and have a vast vocabulary relating to them and their needs.[12]

Clearly, without cattle the Nuer would be a different people. The Nuer even go so far as to distinguish sharply between oxen (castrated bulls) and whole bulls, preferring the former and linking them with the sacrifices that are the center of Nuer religion. Indeed, the ultimate reason for having cattle is "for the sanctification of [Nuer] social undertakings and for overcoming evil in its twofold character of sickness and sin. . . . The sacrificial role is always dormant in cattle, which in sacrifice are being used for an ordained purpose for which they are set apart."[13]

The aspect of nature that means most to the Nuer is that through which they obtain right relations with divinity. Sacrifice hands over to divinity something that the sacrificer treasures. Ideally, the victim summarizes what the sacrificer stands for; the Nuer have compressed their sense of the world, what they stand for and hold valuable, into their cattle.

Traditional African social thought reveals a strong sense of kinship, the importance of blood ties. "Kinship . . . controls social relationships between people in a given community; it governs marital customs and regulations, it determines the behaviour of one individual towards another. Indeed, this sense of kinship binds together the entire life of the 'tribe,' and is even extended to cover animals, plants and non-living objects . . . . Almost all the concepts connected with human relationship can be understood and interpreted through the kinship system."[14]

---

[12] E. E. Evans-Pritchard, *Nuer Religion* (New York: Oxford University Press, 1974), 248.

[13] Evans-Pritchard, 270.

[14] John S. Mbiti, *African Religions and Philosophy* (Garden City, NY: Doubleday, 1970), 135.

Africans have not considered themselves to be sovereign individuals standing apart from other human beings or animals. They have recognized individual differences, but their greater interest has been connections, relationships, particularly those formed by marital ties. For many tribes, it was necessary to marry according to strict lineage charts. Often such lineages were totemic, in that lines identified themselves with certain animals. As we have seen, much witchcraft arose from the sense, whether obvious or tacit, that relations had broken down between certain family members or neighbors.

Most traditional African religious specialists—priests, prophets, diviners, healers, kings—have sought to help the group as much as the individual who commissioned them. Not only could one not separate the individual from the group, one could not separate the present generation from the past. Ancestors weighed heavily in many decisions about individuals. The rites for achieving harmony with departed ancestors could be as important as those for placating the local gods. Tribal decisions depended on this sense of the primacy of good relationships. Kings were powerful to the degree that they carried out their responsibility to lead the people as a whole to harmony and prosperity.

Self and Divinity

Even when traditional black Africans came under European influence, their tribes continued to try to shape their sense of what was fitting, of what they could and could not do. For example, a young man and a young woman falling in love would be sure to run into the expectations of their parents, as the following excerpt from the autobiography of a native African shows:

> A month afterwards she agreed to become my girl friend. From that time I became a frequent visitor at her home. During nineteen-forty we met nearly every week courting. My people in the country knew nothing about it until the beginning of nineteen-forty-one, when I broke the news to them. My parents were no longer alive, so I was in a stronger position to resist tribal ethics without risking accusations that I thought nothing of my parents' wishes that a tribal boy should marry a tribal girl so that she could be a trusted and loyal wife to him. When I told my sisters, aunts and relatives about it, it seemed as though I was speaking a language they did not understand. They all asked me why it was that I could not find a suitable girl in the tribe or in other tribes to choose to be my future wife. They were terrified because she was Marabastad-born. They would not mind so much if she had been born in Thaba Nehu, a Barolong tribe in the Orange Free State where her parents were

born. To marry a girl born and brought up in Marabastad was as though I was telling them that I was going to throw myself into the sea to get drowned."[15]

The simple fact that the author was proposing to marry a woman from the city frightened members of his country tribe. They thought of the city as another culture. They did not know how to picture his future life, since it would not fit the patterns that had governed their tribe for generations. Once again, we see the individual enmeshed in a web of relationships. Even though he lives in the city, enjoying the freedom to make his own way at work, in politics, and now in romance, the author feels the long arm of tribal tradition.

In most oral cultures, parents have arranged marriages. Usually they would take the young people's wishes into account, but not always. The assumption was that elders knew better than young people what would make a good marriage. More was involved than the attraction between the two, for example, family lines. In the smoothest arrangements the parents knew that the potential spouse's relatives were good people. Situations in which the man and woman came from different tribal traditions caused much unease. How would they understand one another? How would relatives on one side be confident they could trust the son- or daughter-in-law from the other side, to say nothing of his or her family?

Within the tribal context one of the best ways to distinguish oneself and so stand apart from the common ways was to claim a religious inspiration. The Nuer prophet Ngundeng, for example, who died in 1906, gained considerable prominence because of his eccentric behavior:

Ngundeng was born into the priestly leopard skin clan and was probably of Dinka origin. According to legend, he was a child prodigy, possessed of a powerful spirit even before his initiation into manhood. At an early age, he displayed his powers by imitating priestly invocations and by sacrificing other peoples' goats. One of his favorite pranks was to curse people so that they temporarily lost their voices. He is said to have caused such a disturbance that people moved away from the immediate vicinity of his village. After his initiation, he assumed the duties of a priest of the soil, blessing the crops and performing rituals for settling blood feuds. But he soon rose above the stature of an ordinary priest. His deeds of curing the sick and the crippled, of protecting his people and effectively cursing anyone who stood in his way spread his fame far and wide. Eventually he announced that a sky divinity named Dengkur ("Wrath of Deng," a Dinka god) was the source of his power, whereupon he shut himself up in a hut and refused to see or speak to anyone or to partake of food or drink for seven days. He is said to

---

[15] Naboth Mokgatle, *The Autobiography of an Unknown African* (Berkeley: University of California Press, 1971), 225–226.

have lived for weeks alone in the bush, refusing food and eating human excrement, and to have seated himself on a cattle peg for hours at a time, letting it penetrate his anus. After falling into a trance for three days and nights, he summoned the people to hear the words of Dengkur. People came not only from Lou country, but also from more distant tribal areas, an unprecedented event, and numerous blood feuds between lineages and clans were forgotten. Ngundeng told the people to build a *lucah kwoth*, "House of Spirit," in honor of Deng. For two years thousands of people labored to build a sixty-foot high mound of earth and ashes. When it was finished, it was unlike anything seen before in Nuerland. It became the focus of large-scale ritual assemblies, reaching far beyond local social boundaries.[16]

The eccentricities in Ngundeng's behavior only confirmed his special character. By inspiring or possessing a given prophet, priest, or diviner, African divinities were thought to gain an existential voice. Often the person chosen would go into trance, and when the person spoke, the voice was that of his or her possessing or directing deity. The deity could make its wishes known through the possessed person. Many of the early native resistance movements to foreign power claimed the sanction of a local deity, who used the possessed person to express unhappiness at the disruption of traditional tribal life caused by European control.

Africans have not tolerated gods that made no palpable difference in their lives. Gods were for healing, bringing about fertility in the family or the fields, ensuring sufficient rain, and, eventually, ridding the country of foreign rulers. Apart from the high gods, who had retreated after creation, usually because of some bad treatment by human beings, African deities were considered near, vital, and lively. People referred to them and recurred to them, whether out of exaltation or depression. The gods coincided with the peaks and valleys of human experience, and because traditional Africans wanted to feel things intensely, their gods matched their intensity. This recourse to the gods continues today in many areas despite the power of Islam and Christianity.

Study Questions

1. What do the rock paintings of southern Africa suggest about long-standing shamanic rituals?
2. How did the BaMbuti use their *molimo*?
3. Explain the logic of the Ndembu ritual called *ihamba*.

---

[16] Benjamin C. Ray, *African Religions* (Englewood Cliffs, NJ: Prentice-Hall, 1976) 111–112.

4. What was the significance of Ogotemmeli's calling Africans creatures of light, emanating from the fullness of the sun?
5. How did witchcraft account for misfortune and evil in Zande culture?
6. What is the humor in the folk story of how the hippo got its stumpy tail?
7. What is the importance of cattle to the Nuer?
8. What gave the prophet Ngundeng his authority?

CHAPTER 5

Native Australians and New Zealanders

Overview

The prehistoric period of Australian experience, prior to the arrival of Europeans in the seventeenth century, suggests that human beings first settled in this area tens of thousands of years ago, perhaps as many as 70,000:

> Between 70,000 and 50,000 years ago, when lower sea levels linked Tasmania, Australia and New Guinea, man first ventured onto the Greater Australian Continent. His journey, from a south-east Asian homeland, was a pioneering one, as it involved at least one major water crossing. The original Australians were therefore among the world's earliest mariners. What a strange new world greeted these newcomers: enormous beyond comprehension, and ranging from tropical north to temperate south. Admittedly, some of the edible plants found in more northerly latitudes were related to those of Asia and were therefore familiar, but this was not so of the animals. In addition to the mammals which have survived, there was a bewildering assortment of giant forms: ten-foot tall kangaroos, various enormous ox-like beasts, a large native lion, and rangy emu-like birds. Despite this terrestrial abundance, it was the plentiful supply of fish and shellfish available along the coasts and in the rivers that drew most attention, and these are the areas in which Aboriginal settlements were concentrated. Regrettably, most of these sites are lost to us: between 70,000 and 10,000 years ago the sea was lower than the present level and they now lie offshore, on the continental shelf.[1]

[1] Geoffrey Barraclough, ed., *The Times Atlas of World History* (Maplewood, NJ: Hammond, 1979), 48.

When the seas had risen, between 10,000 and 6,000 years ago, human beings lived on the new coasts but also moved inland. By the time the Europeans arrived, perhaps 300,000 aboriginal Australians were spread through some 500 tribal areas. The basic way of life was hunting and gathering. Current evidence indicates that aborigines never became farmers. Archeological remains suggest that the natives varied considerably in body type; they either descended from several parent stocks or diversified rather rapidly on the new continent. The first settlers were dark-skinned, and paleontologists conjecture that they carried with them Stone Age tools like axes and blades. The biggest adaptation required was to shift from the skills of sailors to those of hunters and gatherers. "At an encampment on Lake Mungo in southeastern Australia—one of the earliest known Aboriginal sites, dating back some 35,000 years—they fished for golden perch and Murray cod, harvested mussels, and ate small marsupials. But when the rains failed and lakes dried up, the people turned more to plants for food; by 10,000 BC they were using stone slabs to grind such grains as wild millet."[2]

Evidence as to traditional Australian religious beliefs suggests that, across the continent, a relatively uniform outlook took diverse forms under the pressure of local ecological conditions. The people expressed themselves in symbolic terms rather than in abstract concepts, and their sense of reality lodged in their myths and rituals rather than in doctrinal statements. Particularly striking is the traditional notion that personal religious experience begins at conception and continues throughout the life cycle. This notion led to the conviction that people ought to be penetrating ever more deeply into the basic mysteries of their human situation. These mysteries culminated in death, but throughout life one had the opportunity to move, by way of contemplation, more fully into the primordial reality, the "dream-time," that explained why things were as they were.

Among the generic beliefs that characterize traditional Native Australian religion as a whole, the sense that the natural world was originally formless served as a foundation. The natural world lay in potency, waiting to be formed by divine agents. Human beings owe their arising to the work of gods who moved across the land, shaping it to its present contours. The land therefore reflects the essence of the gods or earliest spiritual ancestors. These gods located human beings at various sites, giving them instructions about how to live. Such instructions included the language they were to speak, the rituals they were to enact, and how they were to comport, feed, clothe, and take care of themselves. The gods eventually disappeared ("died"), but they left behind mementos of their presence. These include the contours of the land and paintings on rock faces.

---

[2] George E. Stuart, ed., *Peoples and Places of the Past* (Washington, DC: National Geographic, 1983), 321.

Ronald Berndt, an authority on aboriginal religion, has described the rock and cave paintings made down the ages as follows:

> Rock incising and cave paintings abound where, in the local mythology, mythic beings have "turned themselves into" these: "they made themselves thus" . . . "they left their physical presence" in that form, and with it part of their spirit, part of their real self, *and their image*. Over and above ground drawings, the actual shapes of secret-sacred ritual grounds serve an iconographic function: they represent attributes of a creative being, if not that being himself. Ritual postulants and others decorating their bodies and wearing emblems are regarded as being *like*, as representing, the sacred beings themselves or their actions, or associative aspects. Such postulants are recognized, in many Aboriginal areas, as possessing an essential sacred essence which, through conception and/or birth, makes them part of a particular mythic being, as an extension of that being.[3]

It appears that Native Australian paintings have served as incarnations of the sacred powers responsible for the world. Through the paintings these powers took shape in the midst of human beings, acquired sufficient form for human beings to imagine them and direct actions toward them. The rituals pacing Native Australians through the life cycle have depended on these incarnations, at least implicitly. Those performing the rituals, and those being initiated more deeply into the dream-time, have relied on the depictions of the creative spirits to guide them. Certainly, the stories told about these spirits have also been important, but the visual imagery has perhaps been more a decisive influence.

When people do not have writing, visual imagery—direct representation through works of art or pictograms—tends to shape their consciousness. The spoken word also possesses great force, but in sacred matters the pictured being or idea can be more compelling. European peasants, for example, who worshipped at the great cathedrals gained much of their religious instruction from the pictures etched in stained glass, the statues carved of stone and wood, the biblical themes laid out in frescoes. The sermons they heard made a deep impression, but the images associated with ceremonies shaped their religious sensibility. For Native Australians, paintings of the creative spirits served a similar purpose.

South Australian Traditions

In the Lake Eyre Basin, as in many other aboriginal areas, myths were tied to sacred sites. Along the father's line, people associated their identity

---

[3] Ronald M. Berndt, *Australian Aboriginal Religion* (Leiden: E. J. Brill, 1974), fasc. 1, 18.

with sacrifices carried out at places where their totem, the animal-spirit through which they expressed their sense of their particular kind, was powerful. They would partake of animal flesh sacrificed at such sites. However, aboriginals did not eat the totemic animals associated with the mother's line, as this would have meant eating their own flesh. People gained their identity from their mothers, whose wombs they entered as spirits. In the background stood a Great Mother, who kept in her bosom swarms of spirit-children. These spirit-children descended into the wombs of earthly mothers.

At the time of creation, to which natives sought to return through ritual action, numerous creative spirits called *muramura*, wandered over the land. Among the most important of the *muramura* in the Lake Eyre basin have been a crocodile (akin to the mythical Rainbow Snake significant elsewhere), a yellow-bellied fish, a bat man, an emu, and a rainmaker in human form. Tribes could enact rituals to any or all of these and the many other *muramura*, to consecrate significant sites, reaffirm their totemic identity, and occasion another return to the dream-time. The major stimulus to ritual activity may well have been the opportunity to dwell in the dream-time, which was considered the truest reality. As people aged, they tried to contemplate the dream-time more frequently, sensing that at death they would return to it definitively.

Male initiation rites tended to entail both circumcision and subincision. Circumcision involved cutting away the foreskin of the penis of a young man. Subincision involved slashing the underside of the penis. The word for the circumcision rite translates as "tossing." In tossing away the foreskin, the individual was tossing away childhood, entering upon manhood. Some analysts interpret subincision as a male effort to mimic and so share in female fertility: The subincised penis could be imagined to resemble the vulva, while the blood produced by the subincising could be likened to menstrual blood. Other aboriginal rituals used the blood collected from these operations to placate or feed creative spirits. As we saw when analyzing human sacrifice in Central America, blood is a natural symbol for the currency in which life trades. Australian women entered into fertility naturally. Though their sexual changes required ritualization, they received fertilization and gave forth both blood and children without needing special operations. Men either envied this natural fertility or thought that the basic bisexuality of the human species required them to produce an equivalent. Indeed, for some tribes male initiation rites involved the passage of boys from mothering by females to "mothering" by males.

A fairly representative women's ritual of the Lake Eyre area was the *mindari*:

> A large, flattened mud-mound was made and decorated with feathers and ochered dots: this represented the Emu's body. [The Emu was an important *muramura*.] Two women walked across it to

the accompaniment of singing; then the mound was broken up, while invocations were called to the Emu to persuade it to breed. In its broken-up state, it looked "like little Emus when they are just born." An additional rite of "watering" decorated Emu boomerangs was also intended to increase the supply of Emu: the water was brought by women, who later took part in ritual copulation."[4]

Both these ritual practices suggest the centrality of fertility. An animal like the emu, important for food as well as ritual activity (perhaps because of its importance for food or feathers), can localize the larger problem of fertility. When women act out procedures to persuade the emu to breed, they focus the entire economy of death and birth, passing away and renewal. Thus it seems logical that human beings would copulate after such a ritual, wherein part and whole engage in the same process. Fertility in one part of the animal world suggests fertility in another, or in the whole organic system.

The intense aboriginal interest in the land, which led to a network of songs to fix the names of various locales and retain the myths explaining how they got their distinctive features, plays through many tales like that of Ngurunderi, a leading mythical being along the Lower Murray River. Some native reports credited him with establishing the rites and ceremonies practiced by aboriginal peoples. At the dream-time, Ngurunderi went down the Murray River in a canoe. He was after a huge fish, a Murray cod. The swish of the cod's tail created the bends one now finds in the river. From site to site, Ngurunderi wandered in his quest, naming place after place in terms of what happened at each. At one site he met his brother-in-law, Nepele. The two cooperated and at Rawakung Nepele speared the cod. It must have struggled and carried them along, because it was not until Pultawar that they were able to subdue it and cut it up. They then threw small pieces of the cod back into the river, naming each piece and so creating the many different kinds of fish. Some of these fish have become totemic protectors of people in the area where they arose. Ngurunderi created blue birds from people he met as he kept traveling. At Larlangangel he ran into his two wives, who were fleeing from him. In fact, he found them by following his nose, for he smelled their cooking. They managed to escape him, but Larlangangel is named for his encounter with them there.

Parampari, an evil spirit, challenged Ngurunderi, but Ngurunderi was strong enough to resist the evil one's dreaded spear. When Ngurunderi had defeated Parampari, he burned him up. Everywhere he went, Ngurunderi shaped the land. Having finished with the cod, however, he was now in hot pursuit of his wives. He finally caught up with them as they were trying to cross from the mainland to Kangaroo Island. There

---

[4] R. M. Berndt, 24.

he caused them to drown. Nowadays one can see them changed into the rocks off the coast. Ngurunderi then crossed to Kangaroo Island himself, causing it to be named Ngurungaui. He cleansed himself in the sea, and then he returned to the sky, the world of the creative spirits.[5]

Native Australians discovered that imagining is a kind of being, a kind of creation or re-creation. To tell the story of Ngurunderi was to represent the making of the Murray River. To enact the ritual for the increase of emu was to partake in the creation of their abundance. Many other aboriginal rituals involved making mounds or designs in the dirt and acting out the ways of animal forces relevant to the given ritual, or what the tribe hoped to accomplish through the ritual (for example, a successful hunt). Modern western culture has distinguished more sharply between the imaginatively possible and the rationally verifiable. But the distinction does not settle the matter of what is "real." For Native Australians, living in a prescientific culture, the real was the vivid. If they saw in their minds' eyes the pursuit of the Murray cod, they could feel that they understood the twists and turns of the Murray River, which in some ways came under their control. This sense of security defended them against the chaos of an ultimately uncontrollable creation.

North Australian Traditions

In the area known as Dora-Molonga, in what is now southeastern Queensland, ritual decisions could depend on the visions of elders. For example, if an elder reported that he had seen an eaglehawk, a fighting bird, the people might proceed to enact the *dora*, a fighters' ritual with which they identified closely enough to give it the same name as their land. The people would demarcate an area of the ground by constructing a mound of earth and logs. They would indicate a path into the bush, clearing a space and erecting a platform. Women would stand in a tight circle on top of the mound with firesticks in their hands, then throw these sticks into the circle and leave. Then the initiation rite would begin.

Those to be initiated would come forth, accompanied by their guardians. The guardians would protect them from attacks (by spirits, sometimes personified by other aborigines). The initiands would come forward to receive new names emblematic of a new spiritual status. From the new names they hoped to gain power to fish and hunt more successfully. The guardians would give the initiands the weapons they would need for these activities and teach them how to fight. A ceremonial combat would ensue to inscribe the ability to fight well in behalf of the tribe in the newly matured hunters and warriors. The bullroarer (a noise-making device)

---

[5] See R. M. Berndt, 25.

played a significant role in this ceremony, helping to dramatize the fighting and preparation for hunting. Some tribes also distributed charms designed to help the new warriors do well in battle. The overall effect was to accredit a new cadre of men who could defend the tribe against both animal and human foes.[6]

Initiations of various kinds were the hallmark of aboriginal Australian culture. The accepted way of marking progress in personal life was to hold a ceremony to enable the person to see, feel, and enter into the new status that either aging or the needs of the tribe required. Inasmuch as human time consisted of various stations on the way to a final return to the dream-time at death, such a ritualization made great sense. For women, key events were the menarche, marriage, childbirth, and menopause; for men, key steps were coming to sexual maturity and being accredited as hunters and warriors.

The ritualization of these threshold moments helped to bring home their significance. Ritual changed significantly the way a young woman or man felt. She was no longer a girl, but was now a woman. He was no longer a boy, but was now a man. The initiand had crossed a significant divide.

In the Cape York Peninsula, when a young person came of age the tradition was to separate him or her from the rest of the group. Sometimes a cadre of young men, or several pubescent girls, would be led off together. The mothers of these initiands would protest ritually, lamenting the loss of their children, making vivid the realization that a childhood was dying, and that after the ceremony a new relationship would have to develop.

In seclusion, the initiands would be subjected to strict discipline. What they could say, eat, and do would all be taken from their command so as to impress on them the controls needed to carry out adult responsibilities. Whereas one could indulge children, one had to hold mature adults to strict standards. Unless one could count on adult men and women to carry out their tasks and fulfill their assigned roles, the tribe would fall into chaos. Only at the end of the period of seclusion would this discipline be lifted, and only then might men and women interact.

The puberty initiation stressed the differences between men and women. Oral peoples generally have thought it important to make young people identify closely with their sex. In between the freedom of childhood and that of old age were the years of procreation and practical responsibilities, when sexual differentiation and separation were the rule. Yet the use of the bullroarer in puberty rites reveals an interesting twist on the roles of the sexes. Tradition on the Cape York Peninsula had it that a mature girl had found the bullroarer and hidden it in a bloodwood tree, where the men might find it. Aboriginal women saw this myth as a double affirmation: it was they who had been clever enough to find

---

[6] See R. M. Berndt, fasc. 2, 1–2.

the bullroarer, and it was they who to keep the peace had allowed men to think that the bullroarer was a male discovery. Each of the sexes, though mostly limited to strict roles, could therefore claim "credit" for the good relations of men and women.

Associated with puberty rites was a ritual reenacting the rise of a fish important in the area. A male representing the fish in question (the boney bream) would emerge from a bloodwood tree with an erect penis. He would have been helped to this state by his "wife," a designated female. The notion was that his potency would ensure a great supply of fish. The rituals concerning the sexes brought the goal of fertility to the forefront of young men's and women's attentions. They stimulated reflections on and imaginative associations with the fertility of nature itself.

In the north central areas of Australia, the ritual of the *kulama*, or yam, "regarded as a dangerous-sacred plant," focused concerns about vegetative fertility:

> The rituals are commenced toward the end of the wet season. The yams are gathered and kept in a special shelter. Later they are pre-pared, cooked, rubbed on the bodies of male and female partici-pants, and finally eaten. The ritual sequences include much singing and dancing, body decoration, and a number of subsidiary actions. . . [S]mall portions of the . . . [yam] are chewed and spat out to make the *mopaditi* (spirits of the dead) sick so that they will leave the *kulama*. In another rite, water from a bark container is squirted into the air to imitate rain, along with the sound of thun-der; or a bark basket is hit to make the same sound. . . . Once the *kulama* are removed from ovens and cut up, they are rubbed on the bodies of men, women, and children. Men slice some of them and mash them with red-ocher, rubbing this substance into their hair and over their bodies. Tiwi [a tribe] believe that this prevents sick-ness, and that rubbing in general is physically strengthening . . . Initiands are decorated with cane rings, hair-string belts and goose-feather balls. Although the tangible, visible focus is on yams, it is obvious that these stand for or symbolize a range of natural phe-nomena, some of which are expressly stated, others merely implied. It is as if the dangerous-sacred yam has the power which triggers off the monsoonal period and stimulates all growth."[7]

The yam, a food important to the tribe, is sacred because of its nour-ishing qualities. By rubbing the yam paste on themselves, men and women share in the plant's vitality and defend themselves against sick-ness, which could hinder virility or female fertility. Fertility rites seek a power of body and spirit that enables people to resist attacks against

---

[7] R. M. Berndt, fasc. 2, 14–15.

good health, against vigor, against fruitfulness. The ordinary yam therefore becomes something sacramental. In honoring it, native Australians have revealed their need to find and perpetuate the life-force present in both nature and human culture.

Central Australian Traditions

The *tjurunga* is a sacred object important to rituals in "the whole of the Desert region . . ." Although the word is generally taken to mean a sacred board, "the word *tjurunga* . . . covers a variety of meanings: both ceremony (ritual) and sacred object are called *tjurunga,* as are stone and wooden-slab objects, bullroarers, ground paintings and earthmounds, ritual poles, headgear and sacred chants."[8] After a young man has been initiated into maturity, he learns about the *tjurunga* of his own cultic group, or lodge, and sometimes also about those of other groups. If he is deemed worthy to become a guardian of the *tjurunga* of his own group, he must endure a ritual sacrifice: the removal of his thumbnail. After the wound has healed, he goes to the cave where the *tjurunga* are stored. The bundle of these sacred images is untied, and he learns the songs associated with them. Elders explain to him the carvings in the *tjurunga* boards. He handles the boards and presses them against his body, as though to identify them with his personal substance.

The group instructing him takes him to a pile of stones and uncovers one marked with ocher. His father places this stone in his hands and tells him that it is his body, reborn. It will be his own *tjurunga.* The son accepts this gift gladly and offers meat to the elders who have instructed him. (An offering of meat is the usual honorarium for instruction, applicable at each further tutorial in sacred lore, songs, or rituals.) The handing over of the stone is merely the beginning of the young man's association with his own *tjurunga.* He must learn everything associated with it, which can mean an instruction protracted for as many as ten years. He must learn all the mythology associated with the spirit represented in his reborn "body."

The *tjurunga* are in a way portable paintings that represent aspects of the dream-time. Pictures of recent aborigines dealing with *tjurunga* suggest that they have been intent to recall and hand on the myths associated with a given board. In one picture an old man is pointing to features of a stone *tjurunga,* apparently explaining to his younger colleague its significance. In another picture two men press their heads against a wooden *tjurunga,* in an effort to absorb its power into their beings. A third picture shows two men removing two long, thin boards from the

---

[8] R. M. Berndt, fasc. 4, 17–18.

cache where they had lain. The *tjurunga* are sufficiently important to be hidden away, like treasure in an underground vault.

Rock-art, each element of which, like each element of a wooden *tjurunga*, has its reason-to-be, has continued from generation to generation at sacred sites. Nothing is casual or unintentional in these paintings; the individual artist tries to interpret the story associated with the locale in question. At Ayers Rock in the Central Region students of Native Australian religion have found artwork related to the functions of marsupial moles in the dream-time. At the same site, one of Ronald Berndt's photographs shows a male aborigine depicting wallabies of the dream-time on the wall of the rock shelter. Native Australians have a formidable memory for traditional stories about given sites. These remain oral tales, and so can vary somewhat from narrator to narrator, but they are not completely arbitrary.

When Native Australians enter upon rituals, they spend considerable time and energy decorating their bodies. They must put on the lineaments of the spirits they are to represent. For the duration of the ceremony, they must distance themselves from their ordinary, unceremonial identities. Such decorations vary from place to place and tribe to tribe. In Central Australia impressive headdresses are a characteristic feature. These may stand nearly as tall as the actors themselves. In dramatizing an incident from the dream-time, the actors may dance, bow, and weave, their headdresses adding to their distance from ordinary human beings, helping observers focus on the beings of the dream-time that they represent.

In the Central Desert area, the ritual for death includes burying the corpse. The mourners build a conical mound, into which they stick an emblem of the dead person: a spear for a man, a digging stick for a woman. The mythology of death associates this mound with the moon, perhaps because the moon "dies" each month. The moon was killed because he tried to seduce the wives of another being of the dream-time. Before being slain he was castrated and his penis turned into a stone. After death, however, he revived, and this pattern was repeated following his later transgressions. The implication is that the person buried alongside the mound of the moon will also revive. Like the moon, he or she will defeat death, returning to live through another turn of the cycle of leaving and coming back.

Indeed, death itself is not a sudden departure:

> The deceased's spirit . . . which entered his body before birth, leaves it with his last breath, but does not return immediately to its . . . spirit child centre. Part of it remains in a special . . . mourning ring, which is made by a sibling of the deceased and retained by the widow, or widower. Another part remains near the corpse, even after burial. Mourners speak to it, and then drive it into the grave. But during the period from initial burial until the bones are re-

interred, it is believed to wander far afield and associate with malignant . . . spirits as well as with Wonambi, the great water-snake or
Rainbow Snake. On the return of the burial party, the spirit is summoned by the widow or widower and a native doctor, and is attract-
ed to the grave by a smoking fire. The native doctor catches it (or
part of it), places it in his stomach, and uses it as a special spirit
agent in divination. Later he releases it, and it returns to its spirit
waterhole.[9]

Native Australians, like Native Americans and Africans, thought it important to placate the ghost of the deceased person and ease its way to its
place of permanent rest.

Mythical Themes

In the Aranda tribe's account of creation, in the beginning

> all was darkness, a night as impenetrable as a thicket. The great
> ancestor Karora was lying asleep under the Ilbalintja swamp, which
> at that time had no water but was simply dry ground. The soil grew
> red with flowers, and grasses multiplied all around. Over the ances-
> tor rose a huge ceremonial pole, which mounted to the heavens
> and was a living creature. Karora lay thinking and wishes began to
> flash through his mind. From his navel came forth bandicoots
> (rats), which burst through the sod over his head and sprang into
> life. Then dawn arose, spreading light over Ilbalintja. Karora
> bestirred himself and mounted to the surface, breaking through
> into the light. He was hungry, because magical powers had gone
> out from his body. Although weak and dazed, he grabbed two
> bandicoots, cooked them in the hot soil heated by the sun, and sat-
> isfied his hunger. Then he began to think about a wife. But it was
> nearing evening, so he stretched out his arms and fell asleep.[10]

As Karora slept, there came forth from his armpit a bullroarer. This
changed into a young man, his first son. When Karora came to consciousness, he realized that his first child was lying alongside him. At
dawn he arose, uttered a loud cry that woke his son, and taught him to
dance. The son danced around Karora in homage to the father who had
given him life. Karora received this homage in full regalia of blood-mat-
ted feathers worked into significant designs. The son soon became
exhausted—he did not yet have an adult strength. Thus the ending of
the first dance of creation was a bit ungainly.

---

[9] R. M. Berndt, fasc. 4, 5–6.

[10] See Denise Lardner Carmody and John Tully Carmody, *The Story of World
Religions* (Mountain View, CA: Mayfield, 1988), 48.

As the story continues, recalling how the son caught the food they were to eat, it establishes paradigmatic relations with animals such as the bandicoot and the wallaby. The wallaby, injured and in danger of being killed, astonished Karora and his son by singing a song to the effect that he was a person just as they were and so should not be treated badly. As they contemplated this, stunned, the wallaby limped away. Karora brought forth more sons from his armpit, more hunting and discovery ensued, and slowly the basic patterns of Aranda life were established.

The wallaby's song, like the songs that Native Australians have used to name their territories and keep the spiritual history of each site in mind,[11] and also like the songs of shamans in other parts of the world, suggests how dramatic or ceremonial was the typical oral tribe's sense of both the beginning time, when creation arose, and current time, when people were trying to stay in contact with their origins. Ceremony was the real time. To deal with the original beings in ceremonial ecstasy was to find what one had been made for. In contrast, unceremonial, ordinary human time had to be endured. The richest life was that in which people could focus most of their energy on "dreaming": living imaginatively in the original time, when the world was fresh and right.

If dealing with the time of creation through dreaming has been a major aboriginal theme, contemplating the Rainbow Snake has been an important subtheme. Across the entire Australian continent, the Rainbow Snake has been a powerful deity, so much so that some scholars consider it the aboriginal God. Thus A. R. Radcliffe-Brown, a leading early scholar of aboriginal Australian cultures, gave the opinion that the Rainbow Snake was "perhaps the most important nature-deity . . . the most important representation of the creative and destructive power of nature, principally in connection with rain and water."[12]

The Rainbow Snake has been associated with waterfalls, smallpox, and threats to human survival. If one approached the home of the Rainbow Snake, whether knowingly or unawares, one risked being eaten alive. The Rainbow Snake has functioned in the initiation rites of many tribes, and it appears in many rock-paintings and *tjurunga*. For example, a drawing of a Rainbow Snake found in the Northern Territory shows him being ridden by native healers.[13] The obvious inference is that those who deal with sickness and death depend on his power. He is the lord of life and death. The phallic overtones of the serpent probably contribute to his association with life, while the poisonous bite of some serpents probably contributes to his association with death.

---

[11] See Bruce Chatwin, *Songlines* (New York: Viking, 1987).

[12] See Catherine H. Berndt, "Rainbow Snake," in *The Encyclopedia of Religion*, ed. Mircea Eliade (New York: Macmillan, 1987), 12:206.

[13] See R. M. Berndt, fasc. 4, plate 2.

The Rainbow Snake has also functioned in the myths that women have brooded about. For example, in the mythology of western Arnhem Land the snake is both a mother and a destroyer:

> She travels under the sea from the northwest, and on the mainland she eventually gives birth to the people she is carrying inside her. She vomits them out, licking them with her tongue to make them grow and scraping them with mussel shells to make their skin smooth and lighter in color. . . . [But she is also dangerous, because she] can be aroused by too much noise, such as that of a crying child, or by too much shouting, too much interference with the ground, the breaking of a taboo-rock, or a person's failure to take precautions at times when he or she is especially vulnerable (by going near water during pregnancy or menstruation or too soon after childbirth or by allowing a young baby to do so). Gunwinggu women at Oenpelli summed up the expected consequences: "Far away, she lifts up her head and listens, and she makes straight for that place. A cold wind blows, there is a red glow like a bush fire, a great roaring sound, the ground cracks and moves and becomes soft and wet, water flows rushing, a flood covers the rocks, stones are falling, she comes up like a dream and swallows all those people. She carries them about for a while. Then she vomits their bones, and they turn into stone. They are still there today as *djang* [a kind of spirit], eternally present; their spirits remain. . . Let nobody go near . . . where they came into Dreaming."[14]

Despite all its attractions, then, the dream-time had its dangers. One could not deal with it casually or disrespectfully. Myths such as those concerning the Rainbow Snake made it clear that the sacred could be lethal as well as fulfilling. One had to approach the creative spirits, the divinities who worked in the dream-time, with clean hands and pure heart. Still, the stories of the Rainbow Snake, however frightening in some ways, carried many consolations. The Snake as female could act tenderly toward her offspring; as male he could support his corps of disciples, the healers, granting them power to cure the sick. The very androgyny of the Rainbow Snake is a sign of its completeness.

Native Australians at times thought of this deity as the fullest expression of divine power: control over life and death. Thus to paint pictures of the Rainbow Snake, or recount tales about it, or enact scenes from its mythology in ritual song or dance, was to deal with the most interesting, exciting, fulfilling aspects of reality. It was to sense the proportions of human existence, its rootedness in the natural world yet ability to travel out of the natural world on spiritual journeys into the dream-time. In the

---

[14]Catherine H. Berndt, "Rainbow Snake," 206.

dream-time, beings like the Rainbow Snake held the key to human meaning.

Maori Religion

The native religious traditions of New Zealand are best represented by the Maori, an originally Polynesian people who apparently arrived on the island about 500 years prior to the first European contact (that of the Dutch explorer Tasman in 1642). In 1769 James Cook, who would explore Australia the following year, established the English presence that would become decisive in the following two centuries. Estimates suggest that when Cook arrived about 100,000 Maori lived in New Zealand.

The basic patterns of Maori religion are those found in Polynesia. Reality is divided into two realms: the physical and the spiritual. The latter supernatural reality has included powers of both the heavens and the underworld. These two realms interacted regularly. At birth the human spirit came from the heavens down to earth to take form in the body. At death the human spirit returned whence it had come. The gods were active on earth; any phenomenon whose cause was not obvious was assumed to be their work. For example, thunder, lightning, and wind; the growth of human beings, animals, and plants; illness; menstruation; and even fear before battle all expressed the actions of divine forces. Art was a gift of the gods, as was the power to cure sickness.

> Another critical concept in traditional Maori religion is *tapu* (a term widespread in the Pacific, often rendered in English as "taboo"). Numerous definitions of the Maori *tapu* have been advanced, some identifying it as a set of rules regarding proper and forbidden conduct, others as a condition diverse enough to cover both the "sacred" and the "polluted." Perhaps the most useful view is that of the nineteenth-century magistrate and physician Edward Shortland, who defined *tapu* simply as the state of being under the influence of some *atua* [divine spirit]. Because the influencing *atua* might be of any nature, from a protecting and strengthening god to an unwelcome, disease-dealing demon, the condition of a *tapu* person or thing could be anything from sacred to uncommonly powerful or brave; from dangerous to sick, deranged, or dead. In the last analysis, Maori religion was concerned with the exercise of human control over the movements and activities of *atuas* in the physical world. It attempted to direct the influence of the gods into areas where their influence was deemed beneficial and to expel it where it was not, or where it was no longer desired.[15]

---

[15] F. Allan Hanson, "Maori Religion," in *The Encyclopedia of Religion*, 9:179.

The Maori attempted to control the *atuas* through ritual. For example, they developed ceremonies to call a deity so that it would become present in their midst for some benevolent purpose. These ceremonies stressed ritual incantations; singing guided the spirits to the desired site, almost as an air-traffic controller might guide a plane to a landing field. The key to a successful call-down was a perfect performance of the appropriate complicated song. In Maori thought the intention of the caller (the use to which the spirit would be put) had no significance. For example, one song asks for the spirit of fury to draw near, reflecting a need for a righteous anger to inspire warriors to vengeance. There was no debate about the propriety of this request. The goodness of the fury was assumed: it would benefit the tribe whom the caller represented.

Maori would also try to win favor with the *atuas* by giving these spirits gifts, typically cooked food. Special ovens were set aside for elaborate preparations. At such crucial times as the launching of a new canoe, a human heart might be added to the sacrifice.

Death, which was especially laden with *tapu*, threatened many dangers. *Tapu* could spread quickly, like a contagion. So, for example, it was necessary to sanitize the tree on which a corpse hung, the people who scraped the bones of the dead person on the anniversary of his or her death, and the burial site where the bones were deposited. Because food figured so prominently in the rites to appease and direct the *atuas*, food was an especial carrier of *tapu*.

We glimpse the possible impact of Maori belief and psychology in an account of a woman who died two days after participating in what she had thought was an ordinary meal. She began to sicken as soon as she learned that a sweet potato she had eaten had grown where a powerful chief had been buried. The burial site, obviously, was a place full of *tapu*, and *tapu* must have been transferred to the sweet potato. Because in this case the *tapu* was negative, a power associated with death and decay rather than life and growth, the transmission to the woman was negative. To her mind, a terrible power had come into her bodily system, and she was unable to resist the conviction that it was bound to kill her.

Stories such as these remind us of the powerful consequences of the typical oral people's worldview. We have stressed the holistic nature of such a worldview, in which physical and spiritual realities cannot be separated. Many reports document incidents among Africans convinced that they have been bewitched. The mere fear of being bewitched can be enough to kill them. Either the fear so sets their bodies out of control that sickness and death result, or they give up the will to live, because they are sure that they can do nothing to resist the bewitchment.

For the traditional Maori, *tapu* could also travel from likeness to likeness. It did not require a strictly physical carrier like the sweet potato. Thus, it was dangerous to draw representations of things or people considered *tapu*. The picture or portrait could itself become *tapu*, and so equally dangerous. The Maori would try to bring good *tapu* to their sweet potato fields by carving stone resting places for the *atuas*. If they accepted these places and chose to dwell in the field, farmers could expect good crops.

In dozens of other ways, Maori labored to control *tapu* and the *atuas*. Every significant happening, from sickness to the construction of new homes or canoes, came under the influence of the spirits. The spirits were the agents of the disease, the true builders of the house or canoe, the force that made the crops grow, made children develop into adults, and guided the growth and increase of the animals. The Maori, like most oral peoples, possess a sense of awe at creativity and destructiveness. The imagination of oral peoples is called upon to respond fittingly to a more-than-human power.

We should note the special role that many tribes assigned women in rituals designed to dispel undesirable *tapu*:

> A war party might be released from *tapu* by a rite in which a woman would eat the ear of the first enemy they had killed. A newly constructed house could be rendered *noa* [safe, benign] by a ceremony in which a woman stepped over the threshold. Women had to be careful of their movements because they might inadvertently dispel beneficial *tapu*. The arrival of a woman at the site could spoil the construction of a house or canoe, drive cockles from a beach or birds from the forest, blight sweet potatoes in a garden, even stop the black mud that was used to dye flax from "growing." These female powers were intensified during menstruation.[16]

According to one theory, women had such influence because they were the gateway between the two realms of existence, the physical and the spiritual. The *atuas* could enter the physical sphere of human beings through the female genitalia. Thus the arrival of an *atua* through this gateway was a kind of birth. But because this arrival could happen at any time women had to be careful to follow the conventions for avoiding what might attract the *atuas* to enter them.

Myths and Rituals about Nature and Society

In his summary of the characteristic traits of the various geographical subdivisions of native Australia, Ronald Berndt identifies four areas, each with a distinctive approach to the life cycle and religious ritual. Fertility cults, adaptive and mobile, distinguish the north-central region, of which Arnhem Land is the geographical indicator. These cults stress the complementarity of male and female attributes. The two sexes represent two lines of descent and so two ties to the land, the one patrilineal, the other

---

[16] Hanson, 180.

matrilineal. From this north-central hub, concern for fertility seems to have moved out to other locales to become trans-tribal. The local attributes of both the people and the landscape tend to shape given fertility cults, but the idea of male-female complementarity, as a way of naming the land, the ancestors who formed it, and other key aspects of traditional Australian belief, is relatively constant throughout most of the continent.

The central and western regions are characterized by what Berndt calls a "segmentary" religious complex. The people associate myths with their local descent groups. Those in the eastern part of this region tend to formalize such association more than do those in the western part. Tribes in the central desert area show some of the greatest concern for lines of descent, keeping well ordered the songs in which the ancestors and their places are recorded, and monitoring the exactness of the rituals. The male line of descent has higher status and so determines a greater part of the ritual and mythology than the female. Among the Aranda the key relation is between fathers and sons. Among other groups differences in dialect are taken as quite significant, resulting in peculiar, local twists on myths and rituals.

In the southeastern part of the continent, one finds the greatest interest in magical dimensions of myth and ritual. This is an area where shamanic religious specialists, considered especially adept at entering the dream-time and as curers, have thrived. Supernatural spirits abound and appear more distinct from human beings than is the case in other geographical areas. Inhabitants of the region seek a special relationship with the Sky World, where the supernatural beings dwell.

The northeastern part of the continent displays a cult of ancestors. The spirits of the deceased play a major role in the local mythology and dominate ritual activity. The distinction between human ancestors and creative divine spirits tends to fade; both are dealt with at special sites, where they are remembered (perhaps reexperienced) as shaping the contours of the landscape. Rituals at such sites also seek the increase of the tribe and the animals on which it depends, and other aspects of the fertility of the region.

Concerning the life cycle, despite regional variations native Australians have typically ritualized each significant phase of human maturation. Each ritual affords an opportunity to enter more deeply into the tribe's lore about the dream-time. In describing the convictions with which aborigines begin ritualizing the life cycle, Berndt writes: "Spirit children are, essentially, the intermediaries who bring life from out of the Dreaming, conferring this precious substance upon Aboriginal man as on all natural species. The Dreaming is the source of all life, and anything which touches it is by definition sacred. Sacredness is, therefore, a condition of living."[17]

---

[17] R. M. Berndt, fasc. 4, 24.

In Arnhem Land tribes tend to think that only when one has died can one return to the dream-time profoundly enough to gain immortality. Residence in the Land of the Dead is the way to claim once and for all the natural sacredness of existence. Ritual merely simulates this natural sacredness. No matter how earnest or exact the religious rituals may be, they cannot substitute for the immortality possible after death. In the central areas dominated by the desert, views are not as drastic. One does not have to die to gain immortality; the creative spirits show more desire to enter living human affairs. Because the mythical ancestors come into the tribe's midst, the living members of the tribe can become immortalized, sacralized. The most powerful localization of the ancestral divinities, however, is the *tjurunga*, which therefore serve as the special focus of religious veneration.

Between birth and death, the privileged human occupation is learning about sacredness, becoming sacred. This occurs through rituals, and both men and women are expected to become more possessed by such sacredness as they mature, more taken over by the dream-time. Because sacredness and the dream-time have close ties with fertility, many of the rituals stress fertility, health, and sexuality. Initiation into adulthood becomes a rebirth after a ritual death. The person is new, and this newness represents an increase in sacredness, an advance toward full immortalization—vitality so powerful that it resists death (and so has the status of a creative divine spirit or hallowed ancestor).

In the northern and western parts of the continent, aboriginal rituals are clearest as to the link between fertility and immortality. Here the ritual cycle depicts existence (that of all creatures, plant and animal as well as human) as a great cycle of birth, death, and rebirth. Things decay, revive, decay again, revive again. The local rituals aim at ensuring that this process continues. One cannot escape the process definitively because the immortal ancestors are part of the process. Their vitality is the source of the positive side of the ongoing cycle: birth and revival come through their agency, which the rituals stimulate.

The Native Australian view of nature is distinctively passionate about relations between fertility and the local features of the land. Rituals that celebrate how a given locale came to be as it is entail a petition to make the given locale fruitful and prosperous. But the rituals are more than pragmatic: they seek the flourishing of nature as a good in itself, for what lives, flourishes, increases, and multiplies is sacred.

The typical Native Australian tribe has defined itself in terms of the ancestors who formed its locale and abide with it in present times. These holy beings "explain" the organization of the world, and ritual contact with them gives the tribe its center. From rock paintings to *tjurunga*, the artworks reminding people of the creative spirits, giving the creative spirits a presence in the people's midst, serve a crucial function. Without them the sacred might seem merely imaginary. The artworks reflect the typical tribe's concern to trace its bloodlines, the history of its residence in the places it considers home, and the source of its rituals. They memorialize what the tribe has thought about itself; contemplating them stimulates the people's memory and facilitates entry into the dream-time.

Self and Divinity

Among the Wiradjuri of southeastern Australia, the medicine man enters upon his vocation dramatically. As described by Mircea Eliade, the first event in the initiation of a young man destined to become a healer is for his father to place two large quartz crystals against his chest. This operation, like the others of the initiation, occurs in an ecstatic state, such that the boy takes as factual the explanations given him by his elders. The elders show him that the quartz crystals have disappeared into his chest, promising that their presence in him will make him clever. He will be able to "bring things up"—things that have entered the bodies of sick people and need to be removed; things lying below consciousness, holding the secret to wisdom. Some crystals feel warm, but others that the elders give the boy look like ice and taste sweet. One of the signs of their efficacy is that from this time onward the initiand can see ghosts.

At the time of his puberty rites, the young man has a tooth knocked out. This requires him to endure suffering, and so come to know the sufferings of those he will heal. It also marks him in a permanent way: the missing tooth will always remind him of his calling and the initiations through which he entered upon it. He learns to go down into the earth to find crystals for himself. He is mastering the techniques of travel necessary for this and other voyages. Quartz crystals will be one of his principal instruments. He must learn how to replenish his stock. He must also become familiar with the underearth and the powers that dwell there. Such a familiarity can only help him when he has to deal with the dying, or when he ventures to fearsome spots in the landscape where creative spirits emerge from the underearth.

The initiand is next taken to a grave. There he submits to a massage by a dead man. This, too, is designed to make him clever—attuned to the forces of death and life, expert in the powers involved in healing and helping his people. From the dead man the initiand receives a tiger snake to serve as his personal totem. In the background is the myth of the Rainbow Snake, the archetypal serpent, which he has heard recited since boyhood. The boy and his father (who is also a follower of the tiger snake, and so is delighted to find that his son will continue this spiritual lineage) allow the tiger snake to lead them through the landscape, where they discover the dwellings of various useful gods. The snake is an intermediary between them and these gods, a medium for making contact and communicating.

The climax of this phase of the initiation occurs when the snake leads the pair to the place of the great god Baiame. There they find a thread, which they mount to the sky. They see Baiame, who looks like an old man with a long beard. From his shoulders project two great quartz crystals. Evidently he will function as the patron of this boy's work of healing. The association between him and the crystals sanctions the boy's belief that the crystals will give him the power to be an effective medicine man. The thread to the sky reminds us of the motif of oral cultures that the great gods once were intimate with earth but have withdrawn. The thread is a relic of ancient times, and a pledge that the divine forces have not abandoned the earth. One can still make contact with them in time of need.[18]

In the context of a discussion of mythologies of the hunt, Joseph Campbell has examined an account of a native Australian expedition to a site indicative of the mythology of the dream time.

> In silence, Aranda elders lead young men on a day's journey away from the ordinary camp, out to the sacred sites in the wilderness. Their goal is a cave where *tjurunga* are stored. The elders retrieve the *tjurunga*, unwrap them, and sing the songs related to them, recalling the history of the scenes they depict. The leader takes up each *tjurunga* in turn, chants the words appropriate to it, and hands it around for inspection. Each man presses the *tjurunga* affectionately to his body, and then passes it on to his neighbour. All the while the traditional song reechoes from the steep mountain wall. It requires much explanation. It contains a great number of obsolete and obscure words, which, furthermore, have been dismembered and had their component parts re-grouped in the chant-verses for metrical purposes. This re-grouping of the dismembered parts effectively prevents the uninitiated from being able to understand any portion of the chant when it is being sung. Yet it is upon this old traditional chant, the words of which are jealously guarded, that the whole of the Ulamba myth [sacred to the Aranda] is based. Accordingly, the leader, while teaching the younger men the sacred chant in its traditional form, has to spend much time in explaining each verse of the song after it has been memorized. . .
>
> [After a day of such instruction] they gather around the old leader once more, and begin to decorate themselves under his guidance for a ceremony in remembrance of the Ulamba ancestor, whose life story they have heard that afternoon. The ceremony which is now enacted is intimately connected with the chant and the myth: it is, in short, the dramatic representation of one of the many memorable events in the myth centering around the person of the ances-

---

[18] See Mircea Eliade, *From Primitives to Zen* (New York: Harper & Row, 1967), 424. See also his *Australian Religions* (Ithaca, NY: Cornell University Press, 1973).

tor. The actors wear a traditional ceremonial pattern [of designs painted onto their skin] in conformity with the scene of the dramatized incident; for the Ulamba chief is stated to have worn a different decorative pattern at each of the many places which he visited on his travels.[19]

For Native Australians the self has been a being that could move into the dream-time, deal with ancestral divinities, and draw both power and meaning from such movement. Although records of dramatic ecstasies are few, and although Australia does not seem to have been a place where hallucinogenic drugs were prominent, the imaginative journeys resemble those undertaken by shamans in other oral cultures. Native Australian singing, dancing, silence, and, on occasion, fasting seem to have been enough to stimulate active imaginations to take such journeys.

Although women's rituals have been harder to observe, recent research has indicated that Australian women have enjoyed parallel ceremonial lives, in their case structured by such dramatic events as the onset of menstruation and the experience of giving birth. For both sexes the view of the self's meaning has been bound up in the dream-time. Communion with the ancestral spirits or divinities of the landscape gave the self its direction and fulfillment. Hunting, like homemaking, unfolded in light of paradigms established in the dream-time. Eating, sleeping, caring for children, sexual intercourse, food gathering, and other primal activities took their significance from what ritual entrance into the dream-time disclosed.

Native Australian divinity has been more immanent than transcendent—centered in people rather than aloof from them in high heaven. The overwhelming interest of Native Australians has been in the ritual activity that taught them about the presence of the ancestral divinities in the landscape, at places they were to memorialize in song. These divinities fulfilled the roles of natural divinities on other continents. They explained and ran the system of fertility—rain, wind, sunshine; sexuality, conception, birth—necessary to keep nature going. They also explained the system of human lineages and kept it working. Human beings were linked to the land, the human past to the past of the ecological systems.

The accent on fertility that we find in Native Australian religion is not unique among the oral peoples of the world. The dual process of separating yet coordinating the activities of women and men is a feature of many American and African patterns. Perhaps the most distinctive Australian feature is the tendency to sing about the divinity of the land in a sort of mapping operation that recorded in musical memory the stories of how the land achieved its present shape. The present shape of the

---

[19] Joseph Campbell, *Historical Atlas of World Mythology* (New York: Harper & Row, 1988), 1:2, 137, depending on T. G. H. Strehlow, *Aranda Traditions* (Carlton, Australia: Melbourne University Press, 1947), 1–5.

land, after all, was the most powerful sacramental sign of the presence of the sacred in the people's midst.

Study Questions

1. How have rock-paintings and *tjurunga* functioned in native Australian culture?
2. What purposes did circumcision and subincision serve?
3. Why have native Australians ritualized key moments of the life cycle such as a girl's first menstruation?
4. Why have central Australians associated the corpse with the moon?
5. Explain the significances of the Rainbow Snake.
6. How does the notion of *tapu* explain many Maori practices?
7. Explain the following sentences: "The Dreaming is the source of all life, and anything which touches it is by definition sacred. Sacredness is, therefore, a condition of living."

CHAPTER 6

Conclusion

The Sacred

When scholars of religion search for a word to indicate the great passion of religious people, frequently they find themselves using *sacred*. On all of the continents that we have surveyed, human beings have longed to find sources for profound meaning and to live in harmony with them. From the Far North to Tierra del Fuego, from Africa to Australia, everywhere that religion has been an oral enterprise people have sought to picture, hear, feel, even taste and touch what was truly real. Oral people have been particularly dramatic in expressing their longing. Perhaps the absence of texts, scriptures, has enabled them to seek direct encounters with the sacred—to personify it and associate it with power.[1]

Cultures focused on living words, rather than words from the past fixed in print, have much to teach us about the sacred. The longing for sacredness that we have seen in our survey of Native American, African, and Australian religions is a thread back through the labyrinth to the beginning of our search for the essence of oral religions.

Native Australians wanted to enter into the dream-time. They hoped that communing with the way things were at the beginning, with the activities of the creative ancestors who formed the landscape, would give their lives great significance. It would order their days, giving them direction, showing them how to move closer to wisdom, maturity, the ripest initiation possible. And it would make the world beautiful, for what could be more beautiful than a landscape filled with presences of holiness, replete with reminders of how the gods chose to shape the rivers

---

[1] See Carsten Colpe, "The Sacred and Profane," in *The Encyclopedia of Religion*, ed. Mircea Eliade (New York: Macmillan, 1987), 12:511–526; Joel P. Brereton, "Sacred Space," 526–535; and Barbara C. Sproul, "Sacred Time," 535–544.

and plains, the valleys and hills? The troop of Aranda youth who followed their elders into the wilderness to retrieve the *tjurunga* and learn the stories about their Ulamba ancestor were neither working nor playing—they were engaged in something in between: celebration, sacred learning, and ritual.

The Maori, cooking their food to entice the *atuas*, were immersed in a ritual activity whose goal was to commune with the spiritual world, where they located the deeper significance of their lives. Ritual activity took them into a sense of space and time unique to itself. The space and time one associated with the sacred powers was holy, not to be defiled by inattention, not to be treated casually.

When the Pygmies sang their *molimo*, they moved into a mentality different from that of hunting or building huts. When they addressed the forest, they spoke to the best thing in their experience, their closest analogy to God. Singing the *molimo* soothed their spirits, fed their deepest hungers. Their motive was not pragmatic: even if the forest were to awaken pleased, and so give them especially good things, that was not the real reason for their nightly chorus. They did it because they would not have felt themselves to be complete had they not sung to the forest, not expressed themselves as beautifully as they knew how.

In the presence of Mount Morungole, the Ik, a hardened, bitter people, softened, grew more likable, became less different from the delightful Pygmies. The area around the mountain was a good place; the Ik clung to that conviction even when they had lost most of their faith in the goodness of the world. Something special exuded a presence there; something holy required acknowledgment.

When the Olmec depicted the were-jaguar, they were involved in a similar wrestling with the sacred. The were-jaguar, fusing animal and human qualities, summed up the striking, awesome aspects of their world. Here was the swiftest agent of death, and yet here also was beauty, grace, force so quick as to rivet one's soul. If human beings could draw such qualities into themselves, if they could add such animal vitality to their apparently singular power to reason, then one would see something unique in creation. Then a rational vitality, a pure animal beauty coupled with intelligence, would force all observers to wonder, applaud, turn to the mysterious gods in charge of the world. The iconography of the were-jaguar reminds us that the sacred took flesh, gained a thoroughly incarnate presence, in most oral peoples' worlds. The tribes we have studied did not worship a vague, abstract, distant notion of sacredness; what they celebrated was the swift, lethal beauty of the jaguar, the cunning of the most astute tribal elder, the fertility of the maize that gave their children sustenance, the beauty of their women, the coming of the rains. The lives of oral people were full of the impact of the holy, and they experienced the holy in the most immediate, concrete terms.

When the North American Winnebago praised warfare, it was because warfare roused the human spirit to confront death and life, honor and dishonor, what one owed one's people and what one owed oneself. Warfare could be a holy occupation, bringing one to deepest insight. What was truly meaningful in human existence? How did human beings really differ from animals? Was the rage that energized the warrior better than the tender love he felt for his wife and children? Was it simply different? Was it worse? How could both rage and erotic desire be sacred? How did the power of women to bring forth life and the power of men to cause death coexist in the sight of the gods, in the dispensation of the Creator, the holy spirit? These were questions implicit in Native North American notions of warfare, fertility, the complementary ways of women and men. Such notions derived from a consideration of the ultimate powers and the way they wanted human beings to act.

Myth

Myth and ritual are the principal ways in which oral peoples sought to bring the sacred into their midst, tame it, bow to it, and let it order their souls. Myths are stories, sacred tales of the origins of the world, the sources of the present reality, the powers that shaped the land and the people. The great desire of oral peoples, if not all peoples everywhere, has been to understand the way things are. No healthy people lives in denial. All peoples, cultures, deserving our admiration struggle with death and evil, creativity and goodness. These are the ways that things are. Human beings are a mixture of good and evil. The natural world is a mixture of things to admire, praise for breathtaking beauty, and things to fear, outcroppings of violence seemingly without rhyme or reason. Because nature and the gods are ambiguous, mysterious, impossible to control, human beings attempt understanding by way of pictures, stories, estimates, guesses, hopes. The mythologies of oral peoples are particularly rich, for in their stories we see the attempt for a blessed measure of control. This confidence may vanish as new experience reminds new narrators that their stories, the orderings they have imposed on reality, can be challenged. Still, so strong has been the human need for order, pattern, sense that no culture has repudiated mythology. Every culture known to historians has established canonical tales of its history, its heroes, its villains, its crises and triumphs.

For example, the Hopi of the American Southwest have told stories about the Sun, their ancestor, who gave them the power to survive in the land, who ordered their days by his rising and setting. The Lakota have spoken of the Buffalo Maiden, who gave them their sacred rights at the beginning of time, who put into their keeping the buffalo, the pivot of their traditional culture. Fishing tribes of the Northwest have spoken of the salmon. In the Northeast parallel stories have dealt with the cod. But everywhere in North America, from the forest to the prairies, from the deserts to the mountains and seas, native people have felt called to narrate the story of where their traditions had come from, how the world was formed from the sand brought up by earthdiver, how Grandfather Sky and Grandmother Earth had pledged to support them, nourish them, give their lives wisdom.

The stories of Native Central Americans and South Americans have sought the same ends. The Mayan concern with the sacred calendar, couched in stories about the different epochs of the cosmos, past and future, was an effort to fix human affairs to the movements of the stars. The stars seemed serene, free of the passions that so often disordered human existence, obscured clear vision, and made people lose perspective. The Aztec concern with placating the gods, keeping the present, unstable time of the cosmos from careening to destruction, interwove with myths to rationalize human sacrifice. The myth-makers reasoned that the gods needed human blood. In the beginning gods like Quetzalcoatl, the feathered serpent, had sacrificed themselves for the preservation of the world, and therefore human sacrifice was required in return. The practice—however brutal it appears—was grounded in the economy of nature, the requirements of the forces of fertility and destruction.

Africans like the Nuer whose culture centered on cattle were similarly embedded in a mythological consciousness. The potent bull and the fecund cow served as models of fertility, their strength as a mode of defense against disease and malignant spirits. For the Dogon and the BaMbuti, traditional stories served as the bedrock of their being-in-the-world. Their willingness to explain their stories to outsiders indicates a belief in the fellow-feeling of all humans. To pass on the myths was a way of honoring the spirits again and again, of shepherding the sense of the holy to unforeseen havens.

The same centrality of myths appears in Australia. In all parts of the continent, elders have been intent on passing on to the younger generation the song-lines that explained how each significant patch of territory got its distinctive shape, what each area revealed about the work of the creative ancestors. The mysteries of childbirth were centered in the storehouse of myths about the Rainbow Snake, source of so many spirit children, great Mother in dangerous garb. The way to understand the rituals of circumcision and subincision lay in hearing and singing the songs narrating how the ancestors had established those practices, what the blood they produced represented, what the suffering that they entailed could accomplish.

In oral cultures we find again and again that the meaning of a practice lies in the story long associated with it, while the practice incarnates the story, giving it flesh and song, blood and rhythm. Oral peoples have told stories to capture what had happened at significant moments, but also to imagine how the gods had acted, how the world had come into being. Myths are a tantalizing combination of fact and imagination, actual experience and fanciful play. As such, they are eminently human, since all of us combine what has actually happened to us with what we think about it, imagine it to be, realize it might have been in other circumstances.

Our stories are ourselves. Our myths, whether more or less bound by hard historical data, define our peoplehood. So religious myths are nearly inexhaustible resources for learning how a given people has stood in the world, described itself, told its children where they came from and where they were going. The beginning of wisdom about any oral people lies in listening to its stories, lending an ear and an open imagination.[2]

Ritual

Ritual acts out what myths mean, in the process shaping the stories involved, and sometimes altering them significantly. However moving a story is in its own right, it gains a further dimension, a richer and more comprehensive impact, when it takes ritualistic forms. All oral peoples have located the center of their culture, the hub of their explorations of the sacred, in religious song and dance. People who did not sing and dance would never know the true significance of their tribe's beliefs. People who never traveled out of themselves, in ritualistic ecstasy, would never meet the gods, receive the visions for which their spirits longed.

Aboriginal Australians did not sit still at a funeral, inert in their sorrow or sobriety. Rather, they recalled the stories about the origin of death, the place death assumed in the landscape, the intentions of the creative ancestors in allowing death to enter the world. Then, they reenacted the origins of death, its coming to the land, the orders given it by the ancestors, the ways the people had always tried to ward it off, come to grips with it, conquer it through understanding. Rising, beginning to move, forming dance-lines, chanting song-lines, letting the immemorial messages start to filter through each nerve and sinew, the mourners could feel their burdens lightening. The catharsis of ritual could begin, wringing out their troubled spirits, reconciling them to mortality, the inevitabilities and necessities of death and rebirth.

Native Africans ritualized death and also birth, coming to maturity, getting married, giving birth. So did all the other oral peoples we have studied. For each, any significant stage on life's way called for ceremonial celebration. When the Pygmies celebrated the *elima*, they invited themselves to contemplate the wonders of fertility, the joys and pains of sex, the mysteries of femaleness and maleness, the political necessity of cooperation, the stake of the entire tribe in the couplings of its people. By ritualizing the life cycle—celebrating a new birth, taking their boys to be

---

[2] See Kees W. Bolle, "Myth: An Overview," in *The Encyclopedia of Religion*, 10:261–273; and Paul Ricoeur, "Myth and History," 273–282. See also Yves Bonnefoy, comp., *Mythologies* (Chicago: University of Chicago Press, 1991), 1:3–22.

circumcised, saying goodbye to a beloved elder who had finally ended his or her days—they reminded themselves that time waits for no one. By celebrating the moments of fertility and joy, they licensed themselves to hope that, on balance, human existence was more good than bad, was worth experiencing though filled with sorrows.

Human time is a primordial mystery. How and why we age, whether we gain or lose by aging, where in fact we hope to "go" in our temporal traveling—all this remains beyond our ken. Just as we do not know where we came from, in the sense of why our species should have come into being, we do not know where we are going, in the sense of the final significance of death. We only know that certain moments of our journey, certain bodily or social happenings, cry out to be underscored.

Native peoples of Central and South America have been impressive ritualizers of social significance. What we can gather about the public rituals of the great Central American civilizations, for example, suggests that powerful priesthoods supervised ceremonies designed to prop up the Olmec or Toltec, Incan or Aztec empires. The Inca, for instance, did not rule in splendid immobility, tucked away safely in his palace. As head of the Incan empire and son of the Sun, he came into the people's midst, led them in ceremonies to inaugurate the new year, or bless the greening crops, or petition the gods of the mountains for rain, or commemorate a significant day in the astrological calendar, a time of great portent for the people.

Rituals are part of the cement keeping the social edifice standing. Along with myths, they provide ties that bind people across generations, geographical locales, sexes, socioeconomic statuses. In our contemporary American case, the rituals for various holidays reveal the tenuous hold on us of traditional stories, sentiments, and visions. The pale character of American civil rituals, their often apparently spiritless performance, has not caused us to do away with them. We have not abandoned observances of a higher calling, a deeper meaning, a dimension that might give import to our lives.

More privately, our rites for birth and death, marriage and graduation, birthdays and anniversaries offer further windows onto our religiousness or lack of it. Finally, what we do through the liturgical year as Christians or Jews, Muslims or Buddhists, adds further data, evidence, testimony to our current ritual status. We are the rites that we celebrate, as well as the stories that we tell. We are the moments that we underscore, the ways that we punctuate time, the degree to which we dance and sing about our worries and pleasures, our beliefs and dreads.

Native Americans celebrating natural changes—rituals for planting or harvesting, welcoming the sun or bidding it goodbye— remind us that neither our personal nor our social ceremonies take place apart from the unfolding of cosmic time. The whole living world goes through seasons, is punctuated and made rhythmic by the changes encoded in it. Indeed, sometimes it seems that our social world, the cultural universe that we create, is merely a miniature of the great natural universe guided by the stars, the sun and the moon, the telluric forces working deep in the underground. Thus the rites that so many Native North Americans directed toward the deities responsible for the fall maturation of the maize or the spring flocking of the birds offered them a broader perspective on human processes.

To celebrate a human birth, one did well to place it in the context of nature's entire annual process of birthing. To observe a human death well, one was wise to think about the death of nature in the winter and its rebirth in the spring. For everything there was a season, and for every time a purpose under heaven—North Americans knew this long before whites brought them the Bible.

Consistently, regularly, as a control so permanent as to seem a law fixed in their oral mentalities, Native North Americans and peoples of other continents tried to integrate their seasons and needs with the seasons and needs of the natural world. The bird people and the fish people and the plant people all changed, moved along, took provision for coming cold or heat. So ought human people to do, both practically and spiritually. Thus Native American rituals became a frame for the work of getting ready, taking stock, recalling one's position under the stars, on the map of the life cycle, in the human and cosmic scale of things. Thus Native North Americans realized that their significance lay in their ritual integration with the cosmos.[3]

Lessons

If we step back from our survey of the religious traditions of oral peoples of North America, what is now Latin America, Africa, and Australia to ask what lessons those traditions might offer to us heirs of literate, modern Western cultures, what reminders or new ideas stand out? Naturally, the answer to such a question will vary from person to person, but in the present context let us reflect briefly on three matters: the sacred, mythology and ritual, and the equivalence of oral and literate cultures.

First, concerning the sacred, we have suggested that oral peoples were constantly concerned with orienting themselves by what they conceived to be ultimate reality, the realm of the creative spiritual ancestors, gods, or higher powers. Conceptions varied from continent to continent and tribe to tribe, but everywhere oral peoples felt that the reality that meets the eye is not the only reality, indeed that it is not the most important reality. Whether they called the other, often invisible but still more important reality "spiritual" or "divine," they sang and danced, told stories and disciplined themselves, to gain harmony with it, gain wisdom

---

[3] See Evan M. Zuesse, "Ritual," in *The Encyclopedia of Religion*, 12:405–422.

from it. To pray, commune with ultimate reality, open oneself to holy powers better than the best of human capability has been the nearly universal method for trying to ground the world in significance, ground the self in hope, secure the meaningfulness of the tribe and its prospects for survival. Through prayer of various kinds, individual and communal, traditional oral peoples kept the roof of their world open. They held off any interpretation of human existence that would have removed its mysteriousness, foreclosed its potential, determined prematurely what it could or could not signify.

If there was an Other, or if there were many Others, who had more say about the running of nature and the fate of the individual (both after death and through life) than the say that human beings could muster, then nothing was foreclosed. A current streak of bad luck, or even suffering of evil, might not be the final word. Yet good luck or prosperity beyond any reasonable expectation ought not to skew one's sober perspective. The otherness of the One or the Many to whom oral peoples prayed was a constant call to perspective, indeed to "wisdom."

In a few cases we find individuals from oral cultures—most often, shamans—apparently meeting the sacred directly and being dazzled by its power or beauty, so that they long to deal with it for its own sake, quite apart from any practical benefit it might bring them. Usually, though, the prayers and sacred rituals on which we eavesdrop suggest that bedazzlement served a purpose—usually a generalized sense of well-being.

One can say that the lesson latent in this aspect of traditional oral peoples' religious experience is that one cannot be fully human without coming to grips with ultimate reality. Under whatever name, with whatever emotions as well as doctrinal associations, the human being seems to require a communing with the Other, or the All, or the Holy Powers, or the Unknown, or, to use the most common Western code-word, God. Perhaps we need to pray as we need to eat, breathe, work, make love. If we have found anything admirable in the cultures of oral peoples, perhaps it is the idea that prayer is worth reconsidering, that the sacred may be necessary to our well being.

The usual orientation of myths and rituals in native contexts is to the sacred; yet we may also discern considerable wisdom about the psychological and sociological needs of men and women. Original visions supply a common fund of guiding metaphors and images; occasion ecstatic release, so that mundane, workaday consciousness does not become a prison; renew people's imaginations and wills, so that they can struggle, work, and endure the difficulties of the human condition. Our cultures are what nourish our humanity. We ought to thrive in them like sturdy plants in a well-tended garden. Myth and ritual are the rain and sunshine, the rich black earth necessary to cultivation.

Traditionally, people have not concocted their myths and rituals out in the open, as a public, deliberate enterprise. Their sacred stories and rituals welled up from the depths of the unconscious and were handed down by their ancestors who, at the beginning of the chain of tradition, supposedly had received them from the gods or culture heroes. In repeating them, reciting them, reactivating them, human beings were fulfilling a task entrusted to them, an obligation laid on them under tacit vow of obedience. To respond properly to the gods, the sacred powers and overseers, one had to sing and dance, carry out the rites of passage, retrieve the *tjurunga* on a regular basis. Whatever personal satisfaction this brought ran alongside a sense of duty, propriety, appreciation. Not to continue the tradition as the Buffalo Maiden or sovereign eagle had instructed would have been to show oneself an ingrate, or a fool, or something less than human.

The rationalism so important in the scientific and technological aspects of our Western cultures does not square easily with an immersion in myths and ecstatic rituals. The doubts we have about the nature, or even the existence of God, compound the problem. Still, many psychological, literary, and religious movements now defend the wisdom of oral peoples as to the need for stories and ceremonies, arguing that our rationalism threatens to unbalance us. If we take the experiences of oral peoples fully to heart, we may become convinced that, as their psychosomatic and social wisdoms suggest, the myths and rituals of our own traditions can become blessed ways of uniting ourselves with our essence. We did not make ourselves; we have our debts to pay from the heart, the soul, the foundations of our existence.

Between the peoples of oral religious cultures and ourselves lie many differences. We moderns have a different sense of reality from that available to traditional peoples on any of the continents we have surveyed. Yet some profound similarities remain, and in the final analysis these can be more significant than any differences, if we choose to let them.

For example, we are equally mortal, no matter how much our tables of life expectancy vary. We are all composites of "flesh" and "spirit," no matter how various the connotations of those terms. All our cultures mix masculinity and femininity. All have provided for children and old people, healthy people and sick people. No matter how attenuated our modern Western sense of being part of the physical world, a comprehensive and living nature, we have all needed nature for air, water, food, and perspective. No matter how different the social dynamics of small-scale and huge societies, we have all struggled for justice, order, community. Everywhere, evil has been a painful mystery. Everywhere, doing justice to the stranger without diluting the traditions of one's own people has posed questions and problems. Everywhere and for all, life has seemed more immense, profound, and above all mysterious than we can comprehend.

Thus, every culture that we have considered has been equivalent to our own. The struggle to be human ought to seem familiar wherever and whenever it has occurred. In the final analysis, the purpose of studying the religions of oral, nonliterate cultures, or any humanistic pursuit, is to enlarge our experience, to expand our humanity and our knowledge. We can gain a new, fresh, perhaps wiser perspective on our too-familiar problems and opportunities, our too-familiar struggles with the mysteries of life and death, good and evil, the ordinary and the divine.

Can we not wish for wisdom? Can we not attempt to regain humanity's original visions? Being aware now of what shamans and sages have glimpsed, have we any choice but to attempt new visions for ourselves?

Study Questions

1. What is the sacred, and where does it function in your own life?
2. What makes a myth religious?
3. What key moments in time are most worthy of being ritualized?
4. What are the main lessons that the religions of oral peoples offer present-day, literate Westerners?
5. What is the most original vision that you have received?

Index